W9-CFQ-507

CHOBE

Africa's Untamed Wilderness

To Billy and Mich,
for ten years of friendship
and hospitality.

DARYL AND SHARNA BALFOUR

CHOBE

Africa's Untamed Wilderness

SOUTHERN
BOOK PUBLISHERS

Frontispiece: *A giraffe chews contentedly on fresh acacia shoots.*
Title page: *A stormy sunset provides a dramatic backdrop to a lone Savuti lioness.*
Title page inset: *A full-maned lion — the epitomy of Chobe.*
Below: *Helmeted guineafowl at a Chobe waterhole.*
Contents page: *A majestic elephant bull strides purposefully across the Savuti Marsh as summer storm clouds gather.*

ISBN 1 86812 692 7

First edition, first impression 1997
First edition, second impression 1999

Published by
Southern Book Publishers (Pty) Ltd
PO Box 3103,
Halfway House, 1685

Cover design by: Alix Gracie
Copy editor: Marje Hemp
Map by: Loretta Giani
Designed and typeset by: Alix Gracie
Set in: Stone Serif 9/13.5pt
Reproduction: cmyk prepress, Cape Town

Printed and bound by:
SNP Printing Pte Ltd,
Singapore

Foreword

Environmental protection is an integral part of Shell's business strategy. In the 40 years in which Shell has been operating in this young nation, we have allocated part of our resources to the promotion of a sustainable utilisation of the country's natural heritage through a variety of sponsorships and educational projects. The valuable photographic record of Botswana provided in this book will play an important role in developing an awareness of the country's tourism potential, while at the same time emphasising the need for visitors to respect its delicate environment.

Shell believes that environmental concerns require governments, conservationists, writers, photographers and industry to work together to ensure a suitable balance is struck between sustainable development and environmental protection. In Botswana, Shell has actively promoted environmental education through its support of the Mokolodi Nature Reserve, the Khama Rhino Sanctuary and through the publication of tourist maps and guide books. In addition, Shell is a major sponsor of World Environment Day in Botswana which aims to raise awareness of environmental issues through various activities, competitions and discussion groups.

Shell Oil Botswana is proud to be associated with this excellent publication on Chobe National Park, one of Botswana's spectacular wilderness areas. This is the second publication by Daryl and Sharna Balfour with which Shell has been involved as part of a corporate commitment to promoting awareness of the country's unrivalled environment and the need to ensure its future.

Shell would like to commend Daryl and Sharna Balfour for their dedication to wildlife conservation in Botswana. I am confident that this impressive book will provide an enjoyable insight into one of the most beautiful and unique national parks in the world.

Onno M van Buren
Managing Director
Shell Oil Botswana
July, 1996

Acknowledgements

The production of a book of this magnitude requires a team effort far greater than that of the authors alone, and many people and organisations were responsible for assisting us. We owe our gratitude to so many people, whose generosity and support over the years has contributed to our success and well-being, that any attempt to adequately acknowledge them is certain to be unsuccessful. Our sincere gratitude goes to all those who have supported our endeavours constantly over the years, as well as the many new friends who played a part in the completion of this book.

Firstly, we wish to thank the Government of the Republic of Botswana, including the Office of the President and the Department of Wildlife and National Parks, for permission to live and work in the Chobe National Park for the duration of our research and photography. Without their co-operation this book could not exist.

Shell Oil (Botswana) Pty Ltd provided the means by which we kept our thirsty four-wheel-drives constantly on the move, and for his support and friendship we thank Onno van Buren in Shell's Gaborone office. Shell play an active role in the promotion of conservation and tourism in Botswana, and their continued assistance to us in this field is truly appreciated. By the same token, David and Cathy Kays of Riley's Garage in Maun have become friends in the truest sense of the word, and we thank them for this continuing friendship.

Sean Beneke of SD General Spares (Mananga Tractors) in Mhlume, Swaziland has supported us constantly since day one, and he continues to give invaluable and efficient assistance in supplying spare parts and maintaining our vehicles ... and getting parts to us wherever we may be. In this regard we also wish to thank Sharna's dad, Fred Löffler, for his patient, long-suffering assistance with the mechanical needs of ageing vehicles!

We produced the text for this book and made notes and observations in the field on an IBM Thinkpad 350 Notebook computer which accompanies us wherever we travel in Africa and has never given a moment's trouble.

Our film is processed by Citylab Professional Photo Laboratory, Sandton, Johannesburg. We have not used another lab in six or seven years and have yet to have a single complaint about their service or professionalism. We use Nikon cameras and lenses exclusively, and for their assistance we wish to thank Brian Schwartz and Jan Pretorius of Nikon importers Foto Distributors (Pty) Ltd in Johannesburg.

We wear a range of durable outdoor clothing from Trappers Trading Company and keep warm and dry in Driya-bone coats and jackets.

Once again we must thank the friends and relatives on whom we make frequent calls for hospitality during our travels as nomadic, itinerant photographers. In Maun, David and Cathy Kays, as well as Richard and Barbara Galpin; Mom and Philip Huebsch in Orapa; Billy and Mich Cochrane in Johannesburg; and of course, the only place we call 'home' other than where we pitch our tents each year, Sharna's parents Fred and Mo Löffler in Swaziland.

We wish also to acknowledge the valuable support and assistance of Cresta Mowana Safari Lodge, Kasane; Okavango Wilderness Safaris, Maun; Chobe Game Lodge, Kasane; Linyanti Explorations, Kasane (Chobe Chilwero, Selinda Camp and Zibadianja Camp); Gametrackers Botswana, Maun; and especially Lloyd Wilmot and all the staff at Lloyd's Camp, Savuti, in particular Jeremy and Emma Borg, June Wilmot, Lionel Song, the indomitable Kaizer Rams and all the guys in the workshop who unstintingly helped repair our vehicle. The girls at Ensign Agencies in Maun — Ally, Tracey and Penny van Niekerk — did a splendid job of keeping us in touch with the outside world by radio, telephone and fax, for which we are truly grateful.

To all at Southern Book Publishers engaged in the production of this book — Louise Grantham, Kate Rogan, Marje Hemp and Alix Gracie — it would not have appeared the way it does without your valuable input.

Lastly, we wish to record our everlasting gratitude to our parents, without whose love, support, enthusiasm and encouragement we could never have achieved what we have.

DARYL AND SHARNA BALFOUR
Savuti, February 1996

Authors' Preface

Chobe — Africa's Untamed Wilderness is both a visual and personal record of a year spent living and working in Botswana's magnificent Chobe National Park. Most of our time was spent observing and photographing the wildlife in the Savuti region, world-renowned for its fearless predators, seasonal migrations and tolerant bull elephants.

Our profession as wildlife photographers has taken us to some of the wildest corners of East, Central and Southern Africa, and we have spent weeks and months in many of the continent's greatest national parks, game reserves and wilderness areas. We know them intimately, calling home places most people only read or dream about. As a consequence, one of our most frequently asked questions is: 'Which is your favourite park?' or, even more difficult to answer, 'Which park is the best in Africa?'

The answer is always very subjective and influenced perhaps by factors not necessarily related to the flora and fauna of the area, or the landscape, climate or other natural phenomena. Special memories and experiences, unique photo opportunities, and a long-awaited 'first sighting' also come into play in deciding on favourite places.

And how does one determine best? By park management policies, or numbers of large game and the ease of their viewing, variety of species, spectacular scenery, varied birdlife, visitor facilities, or all of the above?

In trying to seek an honest answer to the above, we asked ourselves where we would most like to spend a year, living and photographing in the wilderness, experiencing it in all its moods, seasonal changes and fluxes in game and birdlife. Without hesitation we both agreed our first choice would be Chobe National Park…and more specifically its very heart — Savuti! It may not have the spectacular scenic beauty, concentrations of game or diversity of species found in many of East Africa's parks, but Savuti distils the essence of untamed Africa, the grandeur of wilderness.

Wilderness is Botswana's prime attraction, and Chobe epitomises it. From the bustling, ramshackle frontier town of Kasane, gateway to the park from the north, where four-wheel-drives and safari trucks outnumber all other modes of transport by far, to the remote, isolated eastern reaches of Nogatsaa and Tchinga, the well-watered region of Linyanti and Selinda, and the game-filled plains of Mababe and Savuti — places only accessible by air (with a suitably rugged aircraft and experienced bush-pilot) or four-wheel-drive…and even then with a considerable degree of difficulty.

From March 1995 to February 1996 Savuti was our home. We pitched our permanent base camp, where we could leave the bulk of our supplies and equipment, in a shady grove of raintrees (*Lonchocarpus capassa*) on the banks of the dry Savuti Channel and ventured forth to explore and document the wonders of the Chobe National Park.

Often we would be away for several weeks at a time, camping out in remote corners of this vast wilderness, frequently sleeping under the stars on the roof of our Land Rover as we followed the daily meanderings of our subjects, or sometimes not sleeping at all as we prowled through the hours of darkness following lions on the hunt. But mostly we spent time in Savuti…for even in the midst of the harsh dry season, Savuti remains rich in game, a never-ending kaleidoscope of Africa at its wildest.

We became familiar with Chobe's vast and varied wilderness on a first-hand basis; the desiccated mopane scrubland and teak forests of the eastern sector, palm-fringed islands and grassy floodplains in the Selinda concession in the remote north-west, papyrus-fronded waterways and elephant-shattered woodlands of the Linyanti Swamp, and the twisting sand-tracks that ply the heavily utilised Chobe riverfront near Kasane.

Our year there was the fulfilment of a long-held dream and our experiences will linger long in our memories. However, again and again we were reminded that the long-term survival of wilderness areas such as this cannot be guaranteed without the concern of us all. Spiralling human populations — and Botswana is setting records in this regard — are exerting more and more pressure on wildlife throughout Africa and somehow basic human needs must inexorably be reconciled with the preservation of wildlife and wilderness…in itself essential for the survival of our innermost souls.

Botswana, which has set aside 17 per cent of its countryside for national parks and game reserves, has a proud record of conservation…and a weighty responsibility for the future. While diamonds may or may not be forever, Botswana's wilderness areas are the country's legacy for future generations. We hope that this portfolio goes some way towards enhancing the appreciation of such natural resources in all those who use and protect them.

DARYL AND SHARNA BALFOUR
Savuti, Botswana 1996

Contents

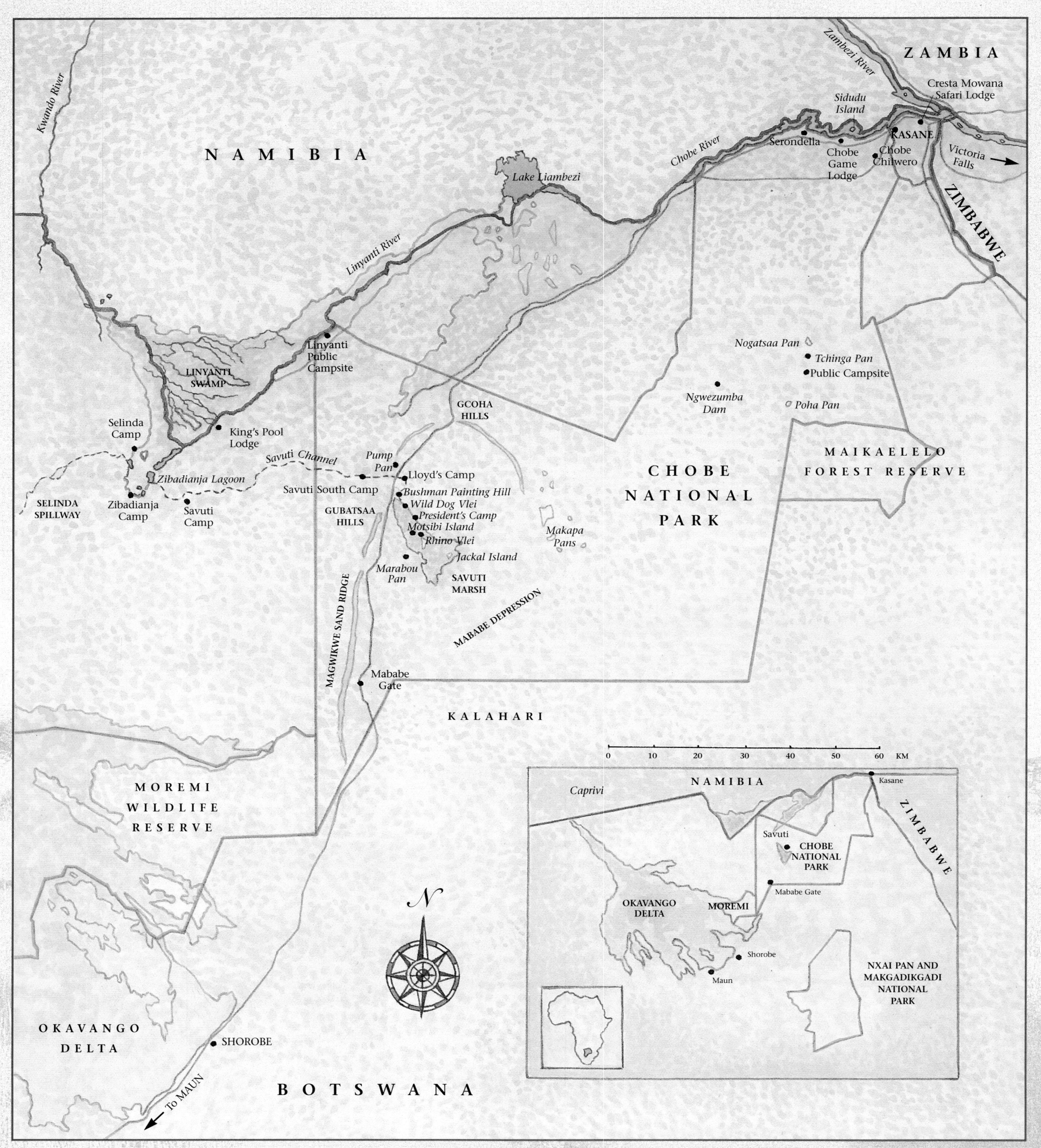
ZAMBIA
Zambezi River
Cresta Mowana Safari Lodge
Sidudu Island
KASANE
Serondella
Chobe Game Lodge
Chobe Chilwero
Victoria Falls
Chobe River
ZIMBABWE
NAMIBIA
Kwando River
Lake Liambezi
Linyanti River
Linyanti Public Campsite
LINYANTI SWAMP
Nogatsaa Pan
Tchinga Pan
Public Campsite
Ngwezumba Dam
Poha Pan
GCOHA HILLS
Selinda Camp
King's Pool Lodge
Savuti Channel
Pump Pan
Lloyd's Camp
MAIKAELELO FOREST RESERVE
Zibadianja Lagoon
Savuti South Camp
Bushman Painting Hill
Wild Dog Vlei
President's Camp
Motsibi Island
Rhino Vlei
Jackal Island
CHOBE NATIONAL PARK
SELINDA SPILLWAY
Zibadianja Camp
Savuti Camp
GUBATSAA HILLS
Makapa Pans
Marabou Pan
SAVUTI MARSH
MABABE DEPRESSION
MAGWIKWE SAND RIDGE
Mababe Gate
KALAHARI
0 10 20 30 40 50 60 KM
MOREMI WILDLIFE RESERVE
N
OKAVANGO DELTA
SHOROBE
To MAUN
BOTSWANA
NAMIBIA
Caprivi
Kasane
ZIMBABWE
Savuti
CHOBE NATIONAL PARK
Mababe Gate
OKAVANGO DELTA
MOREMI
Shorobe
Maun
NXAI PAN AND MAKGADIKGADI NATIONAL PARK

Introduction

Situated high on the interior plateau of central southern Africa, Botswana is, at 581 730 square kilometres, almost as big as the American state of Texas and twice as large as Britain, but is home to a relatively small population of 1,5 million people. This vast, desolate, landlocked country is bordered to the south by South Africa, the east by Zimbabwe, the west by Namibia, and the north by Namibia and Zambia (for all of 700 metres, the shortest international boundary in the world). Although much of Botswana is covered by the Kalahari, a huge expanse of semi-desert wilderness with little in the way of surface water, its more luxuriant northern regions provide sanctuary to vast herds of indigenous wildlife, including one of the largest elephant populations on earth.

A late starter in the African safari business, Botswana has become one of the continent's leading wildlife destinations. It was many years after the lodges, camps and hotels of South and East Africa had been established that tourists in search of varied and unspoiled wilderness sought to find it here. Despite its current popularity, the country continues to enjoy a reputation for providing a taste of the real, wild Africa of old.

Botswana celebrated 30 years of independence from British colonial rule in September 1996. Formerly the Bechuanaland Protectorate, it was in those years one of the poorest and least developed nations on the African continent. There was no capital, no paved roads, no industry of note, no known natural resources, limited medical facilities and only one secondary school. But all that changed a few years after independence with the discovery of the first huge diamond-bearing kimberlite 'pipe' at Orapa, followed soon thereafter with others at Letlhakane and later Jwaneng. Thanks to diamonds, Botswana went from being one of the poorest to one of the richest countries in Africa almost overnight. Today the country has an average economic growth of 13 per cent a year, one of the best in the developing world, while the World Bank ranks the country as the leading performer in terms of per capita Gross Domestic Product and per capita income growth, outstripping even the Pacific Rim countries.

Often cited as a model for the rest of Africa, Botswana is stable, prosperous, well-run and democratic. Unlike most other African states, the country has had but two heads of state since independence, the current president, Dr Quett Masire, taking office upon the death of the country's first leader, Sir Seretse Khama, in 1980. Again unlike many other African nations, Botswana is a genuine multiparty democracy with six general elections having been held since 1966.

Above: *We drive through deep mudholes and huge pools of water.*

Life expectancy ranks as one of the highest in Africa; infant mortality one of the lowest. Yet despite this remarkable success, all is not rosy. Though sparsely populated at present, the country's 1,5 million people are multiplying at a rate of 3,4 per cent per annum — among the highest on earth — and the population could double by the end of the next decade. This in itself would not necessarily be disastrous were it not for the fact that 80 per cent of the population lives in barely 20 per cent of the country, and the reality that the remainder of the land is barely habitable and unsuited to agriculture or industry. The majority of Motswana (citizens of Botswana) live in a narrow strip along the country's border with South Africa, while a further 10 per cent inhabit a small section of the far northern districts. Today there is growing unemployment, and dissatisfaction at the realisation that a mere 20 per cent of the population earns as much as 65 to 70 per cent of the country's income.

Despite the incredibly rich diamond pipes, water remains Botswana's most precious commodity. The country is so arid that the national motto, toast and currency are all the same: Pula — the Setswana word for 'rain'. With rains sporadic, unpredictable and often non-existent, drought is the norm rather than the exception, and growing competition for water, grazing and agricultural land from the ever-expanding population poses a problem with no easy solution.

THE LIE OF THE LAND

The Great Kalahari Basin

Most of Botswana lies within the Kalahari Basin, one of the largest continuous areas of sand on earth, stretching from the arid expanse of the northern Cape Province as far north as the Democratic Republic of the Congo (former Zaïre). Some 250 million years ago this was part of a huge desert covering most of the vast super-continent of Gondwanaland, which comprised present-day Africa, Madagascar, India, Australia, New Zealand, Antarctica and South America.

The Kalahari, roughly covering two thirds of Botswana, is most often associated with dry, dusty, desert-like conditions. People readily refer to this region as a 'desert', but the Kalahari is not a true desert, for a desert is by definition a place that receives less than 60-100 millimetres of rain a year...and no part of the Kalahari receives less than 150 millimetres. It is rather 'a semi-arid area with various depths of windblown sand held in place by vegetation', as Mike Main very aptly describes it in his book *Kalahari: Life's Variety in Dune and Delta* (Southern Books).

There is evidence that the Kalahari was once very much wetter, though today no rivers rise on its sands and only a few flow over them, including the Okavango and Chobe of northern Botswana. Yet in the middle of the Kalahari lie the great salt pans of Makgadikgadi — Ntwetwe and Sua — remnants of a once-vast inland sea or super-lake. These pans, both about 100 kilometres long and half as wide, are associated beyond their perimeters with ancient sandy shorelines and pebble beaches, the most significant of which are two massive sandridges by the names of Gidikwe and Magwikwe.

The Gidikwe sandridge runs parallel to the Boteti River south of the great pans, while the more prominent Magwikwe sandridge curves around the western side of the Mababe Depression in the Chobe National Park, the northernmost manifestation of the super-lake. Over 100 kilometres long and 180 metres wide, the Magwikwe sandridge rises as much as 27 metres above the surrounding savanna, marking the western-most limit of this ancient inland sea, though there is evidence that it extended further west at least once in its existence. Scientists differ on the sea's probable size — estimates range from 35 000-80 000 square kilometres in extent — and it could have been up to 100 metres deep. Most opinions agree that it was fed with waters from the Okavango, Chobe and Zambezi rivers and at the time of its existence there was no Okavango Delta.

The whole of northern Botswana, in particular the north-western region where these rivers flow, is tectonically unstable, and the demise of the super-lake could have been as a result of subtle shifting in the earth's

Above: *Huge herds of zebra dapple Botswana's northern plains.*

crust brought about by the great weight of its waters. Several minor fault lines, thought to be the southernmost extension of the East African Great Rift Valley, underlie the Kalahari sands of the region, though it is generally held that the faulting occurred during (or after) the existence of the super-lake, rather than before. The prime cause of the lake's drying up could have been this tectonic activity allied with faults forming in the earth's crust, tilting the region's surface away from the lake and diverting the rivers so that the waters found a new way to the Indian Ocean far to the east.

Following this movement in the earth's surface the Okavango River no longer flowed down the Boteti River into the Makgadikgadi Pans but drained instead into the present-day Okavango Delta, while the Chobe River (also known as the Kwando where it rises in Angola, and the Linyanti when it first enters Botswana) made a sharp right-angled turn to the southeast where it now flows into the Zambezi.

Further studies have shown that the super-lake could not possibly exist today; the topography and altitude of this region of Botswana is such that the waters would drain off and pour over the Victoria Falls, less than 100 kilometres away. The Falls are 10 metres below the deepest level of Sua Pan, and 66 metres below the highest known level of the super-lake! There is evidence that the Makgadikgadi Pans held considerable amounts of water as recently as 1 500 years ago, although the super-lake was probably at its largest more than 50 000 years ago.

The Savuti Channel — Cycles of Wet and Dry

Nowadays no major rivers flow regularly to either the Makgadikgadi Pans or the Mababe Depression, though in times of unusually high rainfall both areas can be covered by shallow sheets of water which usually evaporate within a few months of the rains ending. The Mababe Depression, however, does sometimes experience unusual flooding in its sump, an area known as the Savuti Marsh, during periods when the Savuti Channel, an offshoot of the Kwando/Linyanti/Chobe river system, flows strongly. (Henceforth, for simplicity, this river system will be referred to as the Chobe over its entirety.) The Savuti Channel last flowed from 1967 to 1981, but since then it and the associated marsh have been dry, a phenomenon that has occurred off and on over the ages. Gaunt skeletons of long-dead trees that grew in some earlier dry period line both the channel and marsh, trees that would have had at least 50 years of dry conditions in which to grow and mature into tall specimens before their roots were drowned during subsequent flooding.

Early European travellers through this area, including the missionary-explorer Dr David Livingstone and his ivory hunting companion William Cotton Oswell in 1851, reported that the Savuti Channel was flowing, though it is generally held that they crossed much higher upstream from the marsh on their way to the Chobe and Zambezi rivers. Two years later James Chapman passed through the area and noted that the channel was dry (in those days it was known as the Sunta or Sonta River), but it was not until the legendary hunter-naturalist Frederick Courtney Selous visited this region in 1874 that records can be considered reliable. Selous reported that the Savuti Marsh was full and that the channel was flowing strongly, but five years later when he returned to the Mababe the channel was dry for half its length and the swamp was in the process of drying out.

Records show that the channel and marsh dried out during the 1880s, probably completely by 1888. The channel remained dry until the summer of 1957-1958 when exceptionally good rains in the Chobe River's catchment area in the Angolan highlands resulted in the channel flowing once more. This continued until 1966 when again the channel dried up, temporarily this time, for it resumed flowing the following year. This wet cycle lasted until 1981, when the channel ceased flowing and the marsh began to dry up — an occurrence featured in Dereck and Beverly Joubert's wildlife documentary, *The Stolen River*.

When it does flow, the Savuti Channel leads off from a sharp bend in the Chobe River and enters the extensive, but relatively shallow, Zibadianja Lagoon in the

Above: *Baboons offer a mirror image of many human characteristics.*

Selinda concession area before meandering eastwards for about 100 kilometres to the Savuti Marsh. The channel is notable for two interesting characteristics: it carries water away from a major river rather than to it, and its somewhat irregular wet and dry cycles.

This cyclical feature of the channel is not fully understood, but it is generally believed that the tectonic movements in the earth's crust, deep below the Kalahari sandbeds, could be responsible, rather than rainfall patterns. Others point out, however, that the most recent drying of the channel coincided with the beginnings of an extended drought in the Angolan catchment area in 1981-1982. The failure of the rains during that time resulted in the lowering of the level of the Chobe River as well as the Zibadianja Lagoon, and, some maintain, the subsequent drying of the Savuti Channel.

On the other hand, the rainy season of 1925 was one of the best ever recorded, with massive flooding throughout the region...but the Savuti Channel remained stubbornly dry throughout, even though the normally dry Ngwezumba River far to Savuti's east flowed strongly! What is known about the channel however is that the gradient from top to bottom is a very gradual one — the channel falls less than 18 metres over its 95-kilometre course. It would not take much of a shift in the underlying tectonic plates for downstream to become upstream.

The region around the headwaters of the Savuti Channel is also remarkable for another unusual water feature — the Magweqana or Selinda Spillway. This shallow channel, connecting the Panhandle region of the Okavango Delta with the Chobe River system, flows in years of high waters. Contrary to popular belief, the spillway flows only from the Okavango to the Chobe. Legend has it that the waters flow in both directions, depending on the water levels in the two systems, but this is unlikely...the Okavango side of the spillway is about 30 metres higher than the Chobe end!

Although there is apparently inconclusive geological evidence to support the theory, the Selinda Spillway could be a surface manifestation of the same fault lines that divert the flow of the Chobe and Zambezi rivers towards the east, a phenomenon known as 'river capture'. In the long run this could see the Okavango River diverted, 'migrating' down the spillway to join the Chobe and Zambezi rivers on their long path to the Indian Ocean far away on Africa's eastern seaboard...an event that would spell the end of the Okavango Delta and the Moremi Game Reserve.

CHOBE NATIONAL PARK

At 10 698 square kilometres, Chobe is Botswana's third largest park after the Central Kalahari Game Reserve and the remote Gemsbok National Park in the south-western corner of the country, but it is unquestionably its most spectacular and diverse, even more so than the celebrated Okavango. To many uninitiated travellers, the Okavango *is* Botswana and until recently, few visitors managed to see any of the remainder of the country. This has changed with the growth of tourism, which now ranks third as the country's most important foreign currency earner after diamonds and beef, and today a Botswana safari without at least one or two stops in the vast Chobe National Park would do an injustice to both the traveller and the park.

Chobe National Park, with its wide variety of ecotypes and wildlife species, undoubtedly rates as one of the great game parks of Africa. Home to huge herds of elephant *(Loxodonta africana)*, buffalo *(Syncerus caffer)* and Burchell's zebra *(Equus burchellii)* and high densities of predators such as lion *(Panthera leo)*, leopard *(Panthera pardus)*, spotted hyena *(Crocuta crocuta)* and cheetah *(Acinonyx jubatus)*, the park is also notable for the visibility of unusual antelope species such as roan *(Hippotragus equinus)* and sable *(Hippotragus niger)*, puku *(Kobus vardonii)*, tsessebe *(Damaliscus lunatus)*, eland *(Taurotragus oryx)*, red lechwe *(Kobus leche)*, common waterbuck *(Kobus ellipsiprymnus)* and the rare Chobe bushbuck *(Tragelaphus scriptus ornata)*. Other popular species such as giraffe *(Giraffa camelopardalis)*, greater kudu *(Tragelaphus strepsiceros)*, warthog *(Phacochoerus*

Above: *The Savuti Channel has been dry since 1981.*

aethiopicus), wildebeest *(Connochaetes taurinus)* and impala (*Aepyceros melampus*) also abound.

Following the visits of Livingstone, Oswell, Chapman and others in the mid-19th century, the area became popular with European hunters, who flocked to the region to shoot big game. Previously the wildlife had been hunted solely by traditional means for subsistence purposes, but the arrival of white hunters and ivory traders, who introduced firearms to the indigenous population, soon led to a massive increase in killing. With 'modern' firearms the local populace could now fill their larders far more effectively... but they were also encouraged to shoot more than they needed to barter for European commodities such as tobacco, cloth, blankets, implements and guns. It is recorded in the journals of early hunter-traders that 10 large elephant tusks could be traded for one rifle ... and business was brisk.

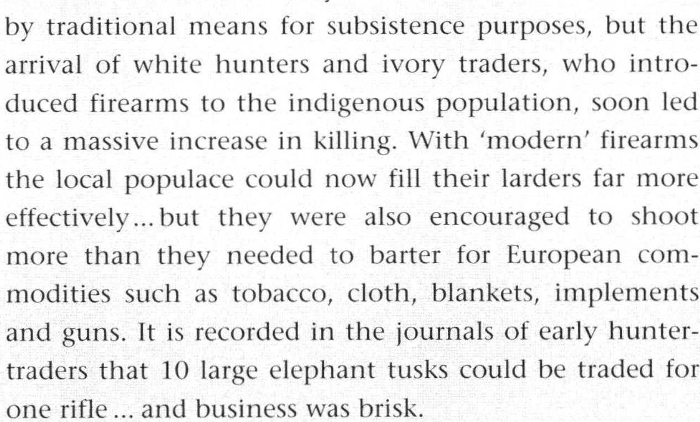

Later visitors to the region sought to exploit wealth in the form of timber taken from the indigenous forests along the Chobe River, and commercial logging took place in the Chobe district for a period prior to World War I and again from 1944-1955. The major timber species were Rhodesian teak (*Baikiaea plurijuga*) and Transvaal teak (*Pterocarpus angolensis*), which still occur in the region in large numbers, although no longer along the river. One lumber concern had its sawmill near the present-day Serondella camping and picnic site and markedly modified the vegetation along the riverfront — something the elephants are blamed for to this day. This sawmill closed down in the mid-Fifties because there were no longer any trees nearby!

Proclaimed by the colonial Bechuanaland Government as the Chobe Game Reserve in 1961 to control widespread hunting and logging in the area, the park first opened to the public in August 1964 and was upgraded to national park status in 1968, after the country attained independence. After the proclamation of the game reserve in 1961 the park's first warden, Pat Hepburn, was appointed, followed in 1971 by Mike Slogrove. Slogrove still lives on the Chobe River and nowadays runs a crocodile breeding station and reptile park outside the village of Kasane. Hepburn was buried in the park after his death in 1980, but his family are still prominent Kasane residents today. The early years were taken up with road building along the riverfront, and trying to persuade people living in the park to move out. A number of homes and holiday cottages (whose foundations may still be seen in certain areas today) had been built near the sawmill at Serondella, and until the proclamation of the reserve as a national park the authorities had little success in moving residents out. But by the late Sixties all had gone, apart from old-timer Bill 'Pop' Lamont, a former supervisor at the sawmill who had his house in a prime spot high on the Chobe river bank. Legend has it that Lamont, in his eighties at the time, staged a showdown over the barrel of his shotgun, saying he would not leave whilst still alive. Fortunately cooler heads prevailed and a sympathetic District Commissioner decided to allow Lamont to remain in his home until his death (by natural causes!). He passed away peacefully at home in 1974, aged in his late eighties, and a simple gravestone alongside the crumbling walls of his home near Serondella marks the spot where he was buried.

The Spectacular Chobe Riverfront

Known for its beauty and vast herds of elephant and buffalo that come to drink from the river in the dry season, the Chobe riverfront is perhaps one of the more popular and well-frequented areas of the reserve. It is also within close proximity to the Victoria Falls and attracts many international visitors intent on seeing an astonishing profusion of animals and birdlife. As a result there is a large cross-section of visitor facilities ranging from five star luxury hotels through fully catered tented safari camps to do-it-yourself camping sites.

Around park headquarters near Kasane the luxurious Chobe Game Lodge, built right on the river banks and the only hotel within the park itself (and scene of the second Richard Burton and Elizabeth Taylor marriage), vies with a plethora of accommodation facilities, tops among which ranks Chobe Chilwero. An attractive wood-and-thatch A-frame camp situated atop a high

Above: *Ruins of several settler homes can be seen around Serondella.*

ridge with a magnificent view over the entire Chobe floodplain, Chilwero has gained a reputation among aficionados for offering some of the best game drives and most knowledgeable guides in the industry. Also situated on the river bank, but some way out of the national park, the spectacular Cresta Mowana Safari Lodge, built around a huge baobab *(mowana)* tree, is the newest of luxury hotel facilities and offers thrice daily game drives into the park as well as powerboat and more leisurely pontoon cruises up the river.

There are a number of other lesser (and more economical) facilities in the Kasane area, while many visitors to the park make use of mobile safari operators, such as Okavango Wilderness Safaris, who offer fully equipped and catered movable camps to create the atmosphere of safaris of old. Of course, for those on limited budgets or keen to do things their own way, there is the public campsite run by the Department of Wildlife and National Parks at Serondella (due to be moved further up the river sometime in the future) which offers basic ablution facilities along with marauding monkeys and baboons.

With most activities taking place along the Chobe River and its vast floodplains, this area of the park is particularly spectacular during the dry season months, especially later in the year when temperatures are rising and the animals are forced to slake their thirst in the river. Most of the game viewing takes place along the riverfront, either by boat or vehicle, and huge concentrations of buffalo and elephant in particular may be seen. Botswana has one of the highest elephant populations in Africa — estimates put it around 79 000 — and many of these make use of the Chobe National Park and its riverfront.

Where there are large numbers of buffalo, especially breeding herds with young calves, there are usually lions, and Chobe is no exception to this rule. Early morning game viewing excursions usually sees a race between the many game drive operators in the area eager to be the first to find the scene of the previous night's kill. They are often successful, but the high density of vehicles in this area is becoming a major problem and detracts from the wilderness experience.

In recent years the Chobe riverfront has also become an excellent place to observe the beautiful sable antelope, while it is the only place in southern Africa where the puku antelope occurs. It is also one of the few places, other than at Victoria Falls or along the Zambezi, that the rare Chobe bushbuck can be observed. The population of this shy antelope at Chobe is in a serious decline due to the destruction of their riverine forest habitat. This is possibly a result of elephant feeding pressure, but the latest research shows that it may also be due to an over-population of baboons, vervet monkeys and guineafowl, which consume seeds picked out of elephant dung and thus prevent their germination and subsequent regeneration of the forest habitat. Moreover, impala are known to eat the few seedlings that do sprout.

Chobe's Eastern Wildlands

The eastern section of the park, about 80 kilometres from Kasane over a bumpy sand track, is perhaps the wildest and least developed, though once the Department of Wildlife and National Parks operated a self-catering bungalow camp at Nogatsaa (now fallen into ruin). While there are plans to reconstruct Nogatsaa, at present there is a public campsite at nearby Tchinga, with no facilities apart from a solar powered borehole that keeps the nearby man-made waterhole topped up and from which it is possible to obtain clean, potable water. Okavango Wilderness Safaris offer mobile excursions through this part of the park.

An area of predominantly mopane (*Colophospermum mopane*) woodland, this part of the park can be strikingly beautiful during the dry winter months when these deciduous forests take on their russet and gold 'fall' colours. Many of the roads can be treacherous during the summer rainy season, however. The Department of Wildlife and National Parks and Chobe Wildlife Trust, in an effort to relieve pressure on the Chobe River vegetation, have established a number of solar-powered waterholes in this area, which are always frequented by ele-

Above: *The affectionate interplay between lions and their young is an important facet of social bonding.*

phant and usually attract a wide variety of other animals, including giraffe, sable and roan antelope, zebra, buffalo and lion. There have also been occasional sightings of gemsbok (*Oryx gazella*) in this area, the only part of the Chobe National Park where they are known to occur.

There is a well-developed network of roads and tracks around this sector of the park, which were adequately maintained when we were there. Unfortunately though, the direction indicators at the numerous intersections were long gone. If we had not kept a close track on where we were travelling and made constant reference to the excellent Shell Map of the Chobe National Park (an essential guide for *all* park visitors), we could easily have become disoriented during our first visit. From Nogatsaa and Tchinga there is a route covering about 130 kilometres (several hours' drive!) to the Savuti region of the park, which passes the old Ngwezumba Dam and follows the dry bed of the Ngwezumba River for some way, skirting a number of pans that attract quantities of game, including eland, roan, sable, lion and elephant, during the dry months.

Linyanti and Selinda: Headwaters of Savuti

The western section of Chobe National Park, known as Linyanti, along the Linyanti (Chobe) River and its attendant swamp lies in one of the most remote and inaccessible parts of Botswana. By 'road' this is a gruelling journey, much of it slogging along in low gear and accessible only in a four-wheel-drive, either from Kasane in the north or Savuti to the south. Guests of the private safari lodges in the area take the easy way in, flying by special charter.

The area is typified by spectacular mature woodlands — towering mopane and leadwood (*Combretum imberbe*) trees compete with a number of riverine species — lying along the southern edge of the vast swamp. There is a Department of Wildlife and National Parks campsite here with ablution facilities, but unfortunately this section of the park has a restricted river frontage of approximately seven kilometres, the surrounding areas being private concessions closed to the public. The Linyanti region is the dry season range of much of Chobe's wildlife, and large concentrations of migratory species such as zebra and elephant can be seen. Linyanti elephants are notoriously cheeky, however, perhaps because of poaching across the river in neighbouring Namibia. The Botswana Defence Force, engaged in anti-poaching operations, maintains a strong presence in the area. Concession holders Sable Safaris have a lodge, King's Pool, situated on a picturesque corner of the Linyanti River. It is managed by Okavango Wilderness Safaris, who offer both land and water outings, as well as guided game walks.

Further west the vast Selinda concession, leased by Chobe Chilwero owners Linyanti Explorations, presents some of the most attractive countryside in Botswana. Towering palms (*Hyphaene petersiana*) reach skywards from scrubby islands that stud the wide grassy floodplains, home to a bewildering array of wildlife year round. The headwaters of the Savuti Channel rise here, flowing out of the huge Zibadianja Lagoon, which is itself fed from the Chobe River. Though currently enduring one of its dry spells, the Savuti Channel holds water for a few kilometres downstream from the lagoon, forming pools that are home to large numbers of hippo and crocodiles. These pools also attract game from the dry hinterland to the east, for out of the rainy season they hold the first permanent water one encounters. The nearby Selinda Spillway, dry for much of the year, usually retains considerable amounts of water after the rains. In years of exceptional flooding in the Okavango Delta the water flows in reverse from the Okavango River to the Chobe system. In other years, particularly if the Chobe levels are high, water can back up in the spillway for several kilometres.

In the early evening and with youngsters in tow, several breeding herds of elephant usually throng to the pools in both the Selinda and Savuti watercourses to enjoy a refreshing drink and to wallow and frolic in the mudholes alongside. Lion and buffalo abound, as do antelope such as red lechwe, tsessebe, impala and greater kudu, while both roan and sable antelope are frequently

Above: *In search of a kill, vultures leave their roosts soon after sunrise.*

encountered. The area has a high density of giraffes, which relish the abundant acacia species that predominate on the fringes of the floodplains, while cheetah find the wide open grassy plains perfect for their high-speed pursuits. Selinda also offers ideal habitat for many of the smaller game species, and regular sightings of aardwolf (*Proteles cristatus*), honey badger (*Mellivora capensis*), porcupine (*Hystrix africaeaustralis*), African wild cat (*Felis lybica*) and large-spotted genet (*Genetta tigrina*) are common. This is one of the least visited and unspoiled corners of Botswana, something the concession holders aim to keep that way. Two small, private tented safari camps have been built, Selinda Camp and Zibadianja Camp, both of which offer high quality wilderness experiences, including night drives and walking safaris, to limited numbers of guests at any one time.

Savuti — Soul of Chobe

Savuti — wild, remote, untamed and unremitting — is regarded by enthusiasts with the same reverence reserved for Tanzania's famous Serengeti and Selous national parks. Situated on the soils of the Mababe Depression, the bed of the once-great Palaeo super-lake, Savuti comprises nutrient-rich grasslands interspersed with savanna woodland with a wide variety of tree and shrub species, including mopane, combretum, commiphora, terminalia and acacia.. In years when the Savuti Channel is flowing, the grasslands of the legendary Savuti Marsh are perhaps the greatest big game paradise in Africa. Currently dry, the channel could flood again tomorrow, such are the vagaries of its flow. Yet each year with the coming of the summer rains — which usually fall in the form of torrential downpours between December and March — the marsh takes on some of the splendour of its former years.

For travellers, Savuti is situated approximately midway along the main route from Maun, gateway to the Okavango in the south, to Kasane in the north. The entire journey is less than 400 kilometres, but the conditions are such that it will take the uninitiated 10-12 hours by road, which is little more than a sandy track. In the dry months, the going is heavy and slow through deep ruts and drifts of sand; but when the rains come, the journey could take longer. In places, especially in

Right: *A Savuti waterhole teems with action as turtle doves vie with giraffe, kudu and impala for its life-giving water.*

the Mababe Depression, the road becomes an impassable muddy quagmire and it is not uncommon for unwary motorists to be bogged down for days on end!

Fortunately, there is an airstrip at Savuti and by far the majority of visitors fly in to one of three safari camps. Gametrackers, a South African-based company affiliated to the Orient-Express group, operate Savuti South and Allan's Camp in the manner of hotels under canvas, while Lloyd Wilmot, son of legendary Okavango crocodile hunter Bobby Wilmot, runs the nearby Lloyd's Camp, also under canvas and perhaps one of the best known safari destinations in Botswana. Lloyd works on the principle that people on safari must see, feel, hear and taste Africa to enjoy the real thing, and has a reputation for delivering just that.

The Department of Wildlife and National Parks offers public camping facilities here too, though at the time of writing the main campsite was closed for renovations and visitors had to make do with a temporary site with basic, but adequate, facilities.

Savuti is famous for its wealth of wildlife, none more so than its huge concentrations of bull elephants and its large lion prides. Savuti's lions have been popularised in several wildlife documentaries by the Joubert husband-and-wife team over the years and a visit to this part of the park usually guarantees sightings of these majestic cats. In addition to its lions, Savuti has a high density of other large predators, including spotted hyenas, wild dog, leopard, cheetah and black-backed jackal. But Savuti's elephants, in particular the plentiful number of bulls that congregate around the waterholes throughout the dry season, are the highlight of any visit.

Savuti has three distinct seasons: the wet (and hot) rainy season, the early dry season, when there is still water available in seasonal waterholes, and the late dry season, which extends through the winter months until the onset of the summer rains. During this dry period, when Savuti is at its most parched, the only water available is in the three man-made waterholes in the area. The first rains may fall as early as September or October, but these are usually followed by a further dry spell, with the onset of the true rains occurring in late November or early December. Almost overnight barren Kalahari sands are transformed into lush, green grasslands and within days herbivores such as zebra, wildebeest and buffalo appear in their thousands. The zebra and wildebeest generally pass through Savuti on their annual migration southward from Linyanti. They sometimes remain here for several weeks to drop their young before moving on further into the Mababe Depression, depending on grazing and water conditions. These herds reappear in Savuti later in the season, around March-April, when they begin their long trek back north to their dry-season range along the Chobe River. This zebra and wildebeest migration is one of Botswana's wildlife spectacles ... and provides a bounteous feast for Savuti's packs and prides of hungry predators.

Although game-viewing in Savuti is an all-year-round experience, during the peak rains the animals are likely to be scattered over a wide area and difficult to see, especially when the grass reaches head height. The wet season is also known to turn the area into a birder's paradise, however, and overnight migrant waders and waterbirds appear as if from nowhere to take advantage of the seasonal pans and vleis.

Throughout the remainder of the year, apart from lion and elephant, the area teems with a multitude of species, with giraffe, greater kudu, impala and tsessebe prominent among a host of other varieties. The wide-open plains attract cheetah and several of the distinctive rocky koppies that occur in and around Savuti provide ideal hideouts for secretive leopard and habitat for the agile klipspringer antelope.

Game-viewing conditions are generally better in the dry season, for the grasses are shorter, the vegetation thinned out, the wildlife is restricted to the limited permanent water ... and the days are cooler. When dry, the vast Savuti Marsh, with gaunt skeletons of long-dead trees clawing the sky, is one of Africa's most memorable landscapes, particularly as herds of game which feed on the central grasslands during the day, begin to move into the surrounding woodland at dusk, stirring up dust against the crimson backdrop of an African sunset. When flooded — and let us hope it floods again in this lifetime — the marshlands rank with Ngorongoro as one of the greatest wildlife spectacles on earth.

Above: *Usually mild-mannered, buffalo can be determinedly vicious when wounded or harassed.*

Above: *The Chobe riverfront is home to the uncommon, exquisitely-marked Chobe bushbuck.*

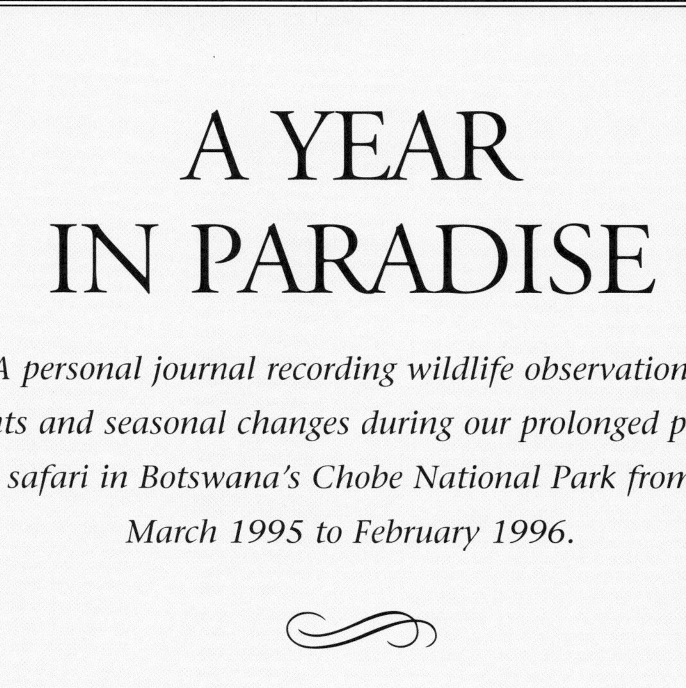

A YEAR IN PARADISE

A personal journal recording wildlife observations, events and seasonal changes during our prolonged photo-safari in Botswana's Chobe National Park from March 1995 to February 1996.

SAVUTI
Soul of Chobe

We point our vehicles north and head for the wilderness to realise a long-held dream to spend a year exploring one of Africa's special places.

Savuti, situated in the heart of the Chobe National Park, is unrivalled in Africa as one of the continent's last untamed and unspoiled wildernesses. It is a place we have returned to again and again over the years, for it has long held a fascination for us, although every visit seemed far too fleeting and incomplete. Now here we are in Maun, a thriving safari centre and gateway to the Okavango Delta, and our final stopover en route to Savuti, 200 kilometres to the north. But this time we are not on holiday, not here for a brief two or three week visit ... we have come to stay. For the next year Savuti will be our home, where we will pitch our tents for the ensuing months while exploring, photographing and learning all we can about the Chobe National Park and its denizens. It is the middle of March, the end of a summer rainy season that has seen too little rain and too much sun, and Botswana veterans are full of doom and despondency. Late that night it begins to rain. The rain still falls the next morning, and continues throughout the day. The joy and elation in the air is tangible, for Botswana is a country where drought is an ever-present threat, and rain (or the lack thereof) is a topic never far from people's lips.

***Previous page:** A magnificent full-maned lion drinks at a Savuti waterhole. **Left:** The skeletal limbs of a dead tree stand out in stark relief against a dawn sky. **Above:** Immature now, this carmine bee-eater will change colour to brilliant pinks and blue with maturity.*

March 24 We rise early to find the sun making a valiant attempt to break through the overhead clouds. After a quick breakfast, we make final checks on both our four-wheel-drive vehicles and set off for Savuti. The first section of the road is tarred as far as Shorobe village and we make good progress, travelling as fast as our heavily laden 18-year-old Land Rover, *Arabella*, can manage. Soon we encounter the dirt, though the first 20 kilometres are gravelled and in good condition. We reach the veterinary control gate and pass through; immediately the road deteriorates. This controversial 'buffalo fence' erected along the southern reaches of the Okavango Delta plays a vital role in keeping cattle out of Botswana's northern wilderness region, although it was initially erected to prevent game from spreading foot-and-mouth disease to livestock in the south. We have left civilisation behind, and though we know the road gets much worse, we experience a sense of joy because only a few hardy souls brave the treacherous passage to venture further north and explore the untamed wilderness that is Savuti.

Fortunately the rain holds off, but we encounter deep mud holes and huge pools of water as we make our way through lovely mopane woodlands to the east of Moremi Game Reserve. Although the track becomes increasingly wet as we approach the southern boundary of Chobe National Park, we make good time ... and the 20-metre tow-rope, which we purchased in Maun yesterday, remains unused!

It is mid-afternoon when we reach Savuti and after introducing ourselves to the Department of Wildlife and National Parks officials, we visit Lloyd Wilmot at his safari camp nearby and ask for advice about the best place to establish our own camp. Lloyd shows us an ideal spot in a grove of shady raintrees *(Lonchocarpus capassa)* alongside the dry Savuti Channel, and we set about erecting our tents and an overhead awning that will serve as a kitchen and dining area. With night falling, we light a campfire and sit back to relax for the first time in the day... then the heavens open.

1

2

3

4

1 *The sun makes a valiant attempt to break through the clouds.*
2 *Savuti is famous for its large predators, particularly lions.*
3 *Swainson's francolin are ever-present throughout Chobe.*
4 *The greater kudu is one of Africa's most statuesque animals.*
5 *Ears tuned to catch any sound, a female kudu watches, alert to danger.*

March 25 It rains all night, dumping more than 50 millimetres over Savuti, but even the rain could not keep the spotted hyenas *(Crocuta crocuta)* at bay. They woke us several times during the night as they rummaged about the camp, investigating this new intrusion in their territory. Fortunately we'd left nothing they could damage or eat outside. We spend the morning in camp getting organised, then drive out to the marsh in the late afternoon when the sun breaks through for the first time in the day. There are huge puddles of water everywhere, but apart from a few elephants *(Loxodonta africana)* and the omnipresent impala *(Aepyceros melampus)*, we see little in the way of game. The sun disappears behind a cloudbank, and we photograph a group of elephants moving across the marsh with dark rain clouds as a backdrop. Later, as we drift off to sleep in our tent, we hear lions *(Panthera leo)* roar in the distance, and a giant eagle owl *(Bubo lacteus)* hoots nearby.

5

March 28

It has rained intermittently these past few days, and when the sun shines the atmosphere is muggy and humid. We spend our days exploring the area, getting to know the many tracks that criss-cross the countryside and where the best waterholes are situated. Every day we notice more zebra *(Equus burchellii)* on the marsh, attracted by the lush green grass that has sprouted magically since the rains. There are kori bustards *(Ardeotis kori)* everywhere, and to our surprise we see that many are followed by carmine bee-eaters *(Merops nubicoides)* that feed on insects disturbed by the larger birds' passage through the long grass. We are fascinated to see that the bee-eaters even perch on the bustards' backs, the 'hosts' apparently unconcerned by their unusual passengers, but we are unable to get anywhere near for photographs!

March 29

A lovely sunny dawn greets us for the first time since our arrival, and we head down towards Savuti Marsh, where we could hear lions during the night. Opposite Leopard Rock we find them, 13 members of the local Sethlare Pride, gorging themselves on a buffalo *(Syncerus caffer)* killed only a few hours earlier, judging from its condition. We spend two hours with them, then head homewards as thunder clouds build up again. The rain buckets down in the afternoon, and lightning strikes two trees nearby, causing them to fizzle and smoulder in the pouring rain.

April 2

We rise early after a night disturbed by a magnificent thunderstorm, thunder and lightning crashing around the koppies across the channel from our camp, but the sky is heavily overcast and we decide to spend the morning in camp catching up on our chores. A band of clear sky above the western horizon promises good light in the late afternoon, so we rush down to the marsh. The promise is fulfilled and we spend time photographing a herd of impala in amongst all the old dead trees.

1 *Impala graze contentedly among the old dead trees that mark the Savuti Marsh.*

2 & 3 *Herds of zebra gather on the lush green grass that has sprouted magically since the late rains.*

4 *The open grassland of Savuti provides ideal habitat for cheetah. Though usually solitary, these two are probably mother and daughter.*

5

April 3 Once again the morning dawns dull and overcast, but we head out down south of the marsh and find a group of giraffe *(Giraffa camelopardalis)* with several youngsters who entertain us with their antics. Later we find a beautiful golden orb-web spider *(Nephila senegalensis)* in a magnificent web, strung between two candlepod bushes *(Acacia hebeclada)*. We return to the marsh in the afternoon and while photographing a herd of impala see two wildebeest bulls *(Connochaetes taurinus)* engaged in a territorial dispute. They chase each other hither and thither, until eventually they engage in close combat. Both bulls go down on their knees, horns hooking and slashing at each other until eventually one emerges as the victor, strutting imperiously back to his herd while the vanquished limps away, blood dripping from wounds on his chest and forelegs. Driving past the old airfield pans, recently renamed Pitse (zebra) Pans, on our way back to camp we see a family of nine bat-eared foxes *(Otocyon megalotis)*, but it is already too dark for photography.

1

April 4 Out on the marsh we are successful in our attempts to photograph a kori bustard with carmine bee-eaters at last. We spend over an hour following a very co-operative bustard and notice that the 'jockey' position seems to be very sought after. There is usually at least one other carmine hovering nearby, ready to alight on the kori bustard's back should the first bird move off. It is also evident that only the carmine bee-eaters have this habit, for there are other bee-eater varieties in the vicinity that show no inclination to mimic this unusual behaviour, even though they, too, swoop gracefully over the grasslands catching insects.

2

3

6

4

1 A magnificent golden orb-web spider hangs on silken threads strung between two bushes.

2 Wild dogs tear the jackal to pieces within a minute.

3 & 4 A carmine bee-eater assumes the jockey-position atop a large kori bustard as it strides across the grasslands. Savuti is one of the few places where this unusual behaviour is readily observed.

5 We find a group of giraffe with several youngsters at the southern end of the marsh.

6 Two wildebeest bulls engage in a vicious territorial dispute.

April 5 Fifteen lions lie scattered in the bush near Leopard Rock, but soon move off into thick scrub west of the track and we lose them. Later, on the eastern side of the marsh we watch three wild dogs *(Lycaon pictus)* chase a herd of tsessebe *(Damaliscus lunatus)* without luck — these antelope are reputedly the fastest in Africa. The dogs then flush a pair of black-backed jackal *(Canis mesomelas)* out of the long grass and manage to catch one of them, tearing it to shreds in seconds as its mate howls and yelps in dismay, rushing in and nipping at the wild dogs now and again. To our surprise, the dogs devour every last scrap of the jackal. We find it interesting that wild dogs actually eat other predators, even though we knew that they would kill them given the opportunity.

1

3

April 6 We sight our first leopard *(Panthera pardus)* in the channel near President's Camp, but it quickly moves into thick undergrowth and out of sight. We drive on and not five minutes later find yesterday's lions lying in a bunch just off the track. They appear to have settled down to sleep for the day, so after enjoying a cup of tea and bowl of cereal in their company, we continue our drive. (We always have a flask of boiling water and a plastic 'lug-box' with basic provisions, tea, biscuits and so on when we set out in the Land Rover each day, for we never know quite when we'll get back to camp.) Near Rhino Vlei we see two other lionesses — not members of the Sethlare Pride — stalking a herd of impala, but they bungle the attempt and give up in disgust. We continue and find huge flocks of cattle egrets *(Bubulcus ibis)* and a lone wattled crane *(Grus carunculata)* near the Jackal Island Pans. We search for a large family of six cheetah *(Acinonyx jubatus)* which others have seen, to no avail.

April 7 Another fleeting glimpse of a leopard, but once again it disappears from view in the thick bush. We move on to Peter's Pan and find 15 lion in a playful mood, romping about and clambering into the branches of a raintree at the water's edge. These lions were dubbed the Sethlare Pride by the guides at Lloyd's Camp. 'Sethlare' in the local Tswana dialect means 'tree', which these lions have a reputation for climbing. There are seven adult lionesses — one of whom was absent, perhaps with newborn cubs — and nine half-grown cubs and sub-adults in the pride. We spend an entertaining hour as the youngsters take turns in climbing into the tree, sliding back down the trunk and generally fooling about. The two big adult pride males have not been seen by us at all yet, nor by others in Savuti for some time. On the marsh we notice that the carmine bee-eaters have left the area, for the kori bustards walk alone. Later we watch a giraffe feeding on an acacia, delicately stripping the leaves from the spiny branches with its long tongue. The sky clouds over in the late afternoon, but the sun shines through underneath, bathing the massing herds of zebra in glorious golden light.

2

4

1 & 2 The Sethlare Pride in playful mood, clambering about the branches of a tree alongside Peter's Pan.

3 When feeding, giraffe use their 40-centimetre-long tongues to strip foliage from the thorny branches.

4 Huge flocks of cattle egrets gather near the Jackal Island Pans.

1

2

1 *Two male giraffe engage in a bout of neck-wrestling, which will help establish their hierarchical status.*
2 *A magnificent male leopard lies sunning himself in a dead tree.*
3 *A family of bat-eared foxes lie huddled together, basking in the warmth of the sun.*
4 *Elephants gather on the marsh to feed on the sweet, nutritious grasses.*

April 9 A beautiful golden pink sunrise greets the day as we make our way down the western side of the marsh to visit a colony of dwarf mongooses *(Helogale parvula)* we found yesterday. En route we see a magnificent martial eagle *(Polemaetus bellicosus)* perched in a dead tree, and we spend some time photographing it, then move on, only to find the mongooses have abandoned their den. We spend the rest of the morning photographing birds, in particular the various varieties of francolins we see warming themselves in the morning sun.

April 11 Driving in an area north of our camp shortly after sunrise we find a magnificent big male leopard sunning himself in a dead tree and manage to take a few photographs before he slinks down from his vantage point and disappears into the bushes. The rest of the day passes uneventfully, and we spend the afternoon on the marsh where more and more elephants gather every day to enjoy the sweet, nutritious grasses that have sprouted since the rains. Later, as we are about to return to camp, we hear a commotion in the thick mopane woodland *(Colophospermum mopane)* to the east of us and on investigation we discover two young elephant bulls having a tremendous battle with each other, wrestling and clashing tusks, shoving and trumpeting their ire. Then, as abruptly as it all began, the elephants turn away from each other and head off in separate directions.

April 13 We spend the early hours of the morning with a family of bat-eared foxes — two adults and six youngsters — who reward our patient manoeuvring, a little closer at a time, by eventually allowing our Land Rover within 30 metres of where they lie basking in the sun. While we sit with the bat-eared foxes a number of giraffe appear and stride across the open plain, two males pausing for a bout of neck-wrestling nearby. As we watch, more and more giraffe make their way out of the woodland until soon there are 24 of them scattered about. They take turns ambling to a small waterhole, where they drink with usual giraffely caution, their legs spread wide and long necks awkwardly lowered.

3

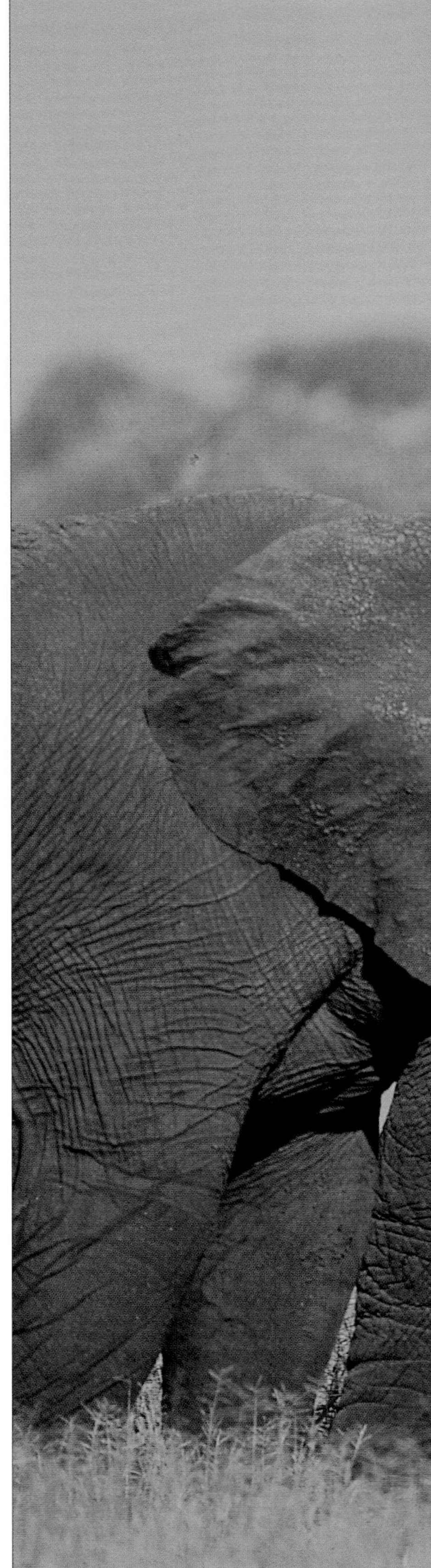

4

1

April 14 We find a family of yellow mongooses *(Cynictis penicillata)* that have moved into the den previously occupied by the dwarf mongooses, and spend an entertaining morning photographing their antics. The den is a disused termite mound, and the youngsters seem to delight in exploring every nook and cranny, disappearing from our view down one hole, then popping out another. As the morning warms up more family members appear out of the den, and they sit about grooming each other in the sun, or simply sunbathing. Eventually they all drift away, foraging in the undergrowth in the nearby acacia scrub. On our way back to camp we notice how many of the trees are beginning to change colour with the onset of autumn, beautiful burnished bronze, gold, yellow and brown. The towering camelthorn trees *(Acacia erioloba)*, a distinctive feature of the Savuti area, are covered with large, velvety seedpods, which are relished by elephant, giraffe and greater kudu *(Tragelaphus strepsiceros)*.

April 15 Leaving camp before first light we head south towards Leopard Rock where we find the Sethlare Pride up to their usual tree-climbing antics, this time clambering about a dead tree that has fallen on its side near the road. Unfortunately it is still dark, but we take a few shots first using electronic flash, then using a high speed film (400 ASA) in the pre-dawn glow. As the light begins to improve several other vehicles arrive and, disturbed by all the onlookers, the lions move off into dense scrub. Frustrated, we drive on, seeing a number of ostriches *(Struthio camelus)* out on the marsh, and we have a bit of fun with a rufousnaped lark *(Mirafra africana)* perched near the road whistling stridently. We mimic its call, and it responds enthusiastically and even more loudly, flapping its wings and preening for its unseen rival, or suitor!

4

2

3

5

1 *Many bushveld trees change colour with the onset of autumn.*

2 *A family of yellow mongooses takes up residence in a disused termite mound.*

3 *Camelthorn trees are covered with large, velvety seedpods.*

4 *A rufousnaped lark perches near the track, whistling for a mate.*

5 *The Sethlare lions are up to their usual tree-climbing antics in a fallen tree.*

April 16 Easter Sunday rewards us with a magnificent young leopard posing perfectly on a fallen tree trunk near Leopard Rock. We have him to ourselves for some time, then a vehicle from one of the lodges nearby sees us and comes closer to investigate. To our irritation, we hear the driver calling the other vehicles from the lodge on his two-way radio within seconds of stopping, and minutes later we are surrounded by vehicles — and excited, noisy tourists! The leopard takes one look at this melee and slinks off into the bush, vanishing from sight. Soon the other vehicles leave, but we stay put, tracking the spotted cat's progress through the undergrowth by the alarm calls broadcast by an alert redbilled francolin *(Francolinus adspersus)*, until he emerges again quite close to us. The leopard stands motionless, staring intently straight into our lenses, before turning and melting away once again.

4

April 18 First light finds us on the track to the southern end of the Mababe Depression, where we hope to discover the majority of the zebra herds, for still they have not arrived at Savuti in their usual numbers. We encounter a courting pair of lions lying at the roadside and follow them as they head off into the bush, passing a sizeable herd of zebra and several giraffe as we go. The lions, intent on their courtship, barely glance at these potential prey, though the zebras rush closer to have a good look at the lions! They lead us to a cluster of small rainwater pools, where they sprawl in the shade of several trees, but though we sit patiently for several hours, they show no signs of mating and eventually we leave them to continue our search for the main zebra migration. Although we search all over the area, we find only small pockets of zebras scattered widely, though we notice that they are all heading in a northerly direction.

1 *The zebras rush closer to stare at the departing lions.*
2 *We are rewarded with a beautiful young leopard posing perfectly on a fallen tree.*
3 *A courting pair of lions near the road side. They will probably mate 2 or 3 times per hour for the next 4 days.*
4 *We track the young leopard by following the alarm calls of a redbilled francolin.*
5 *The leopard stands motionless, staring intently into the lens.*

5

April 21 We find the Sethlare Pride close to the road near Sable Hill in the company of a beautiful full-maned male. The sub-adult males in the pride appear fascinated by him, perhaps their father, and take it in turns to approach him, very tentatively. As they get close they flop on to their bellies and roll over submissively, but the lion shows no interest in being fatherly and snarls and growls at them, swiping out with a huge paw. The youngsters eventually give up and move away, but lie watching him intently, expressions of utter fascination on their faces. Only one of the lionesses shows interest in the male and she approaches him from time to time, nuzzling his mane. We later hear from June Wilmot that this lion is Othello; the other adult male in the pride is named Pandani.

1

April 24 In the afternoon we find two nomadic lionesses sleeping in the bush near the old airfield pans and are about to move on when we observe several members of the Sethlare Pride approaching in the distance. The two lionesses also see them, and immediately get up and run away with three of the pride females in furious pursuit, followed by several others. The nomads manage to escape unscathed and the pride regroups around the pans, roaring and grunting in a united show of force and dominance. From some distance away, the two strangers return the roars, but though the pride members show anger and concern, they soon settle down, drinking, grooming and playing at the water's edge. We sit with the lions until the sun sets with fiery splendour, enjoying the aura of primeval Africa.

April 25 For the past few nights we have followed the Sethlare Pride in their nocturnal ramblings. We had hoped to photograph them hunting, but it appears that the youngsters are still too young to participate in the hunts, and we have only managed to witness a few impala kills. By the time we catch up to the action, there is not much to

3

2

1 & 2 The embodiment of Savuti, the magnificent black-maned lion named Othello.

3 The lion pride eventually settles down alongside the waterhole after the territorial dispute.

4 We stay with the lions while the sun sets in fiery splendour.

4

be seen of the impala under 15 or 16 lions! When following the lions we ride with our headlights extinguished, observing them by the light of the moon and staying at the rear with the youngsters. The lioness who has been absent from the pride joins them each night to hunt, and it appears that she may have hidden her cubs near Leopard Rock, for she returns there afterwards. Only two of her teats show signs of having been suckled, so it is likely she has only one or two cubs. When hunting, usually six of the lionesses go off, one remaining with the sub-adults, who lie intensely alert. At the first sign or call, which we are unable to hear, they leap to their feet and race off through the bush at top speed, with us jolting along in their wake, to join the others at the kill. The pride is killing three or four impala a night to keep their numbers fed.

1

2

1 & 4 Several large bull elephants drink noisily only metres from where we lie with our cameras at the water's edge.
2 A sub-adult greater kestrel perches on a dead tree, feeding on an insect it has caught in the grass.
3 Giraffe must bend awkwardly to drink, splaying their legs wide in order to lower their head and neck.

Overleaf: *Groups of zebra come to drink, wading chest-deep into the water.*

3

April 29 Early morning finds us at Peter's Pan with the Sethlare Pride up to their usual antics in the tree. Later we move on to Marabou Pan at the southern end of the marsh where we find several giraffe and herds of zebra at the waterhole. Continuing, we encounter Othello and one lioness at Gardenia Island. She is not from the Sethlare Pride and we presume she is one of Maome's Pride, which frequents this southern area. There are countless zebra on the marsh now, wherever we look, and large flocks of Abdim's storks *(Ciconia abdimii)* and Egyptian geese *(Alopochen aegyptiacus)*. We return to Peter's Pan at sunset, where the Sethlare lions have rested all day. They lie about, inactive until the last tourist vehicle leaves, then rise, stretch and set off on the nightly hunt! We follow a short way, but when they start heading up the sandridge we call it off and decide to return to camp.

May 1 Rain fell softly all night and there are still clouds in the sky this morning, as well as a bitingly cold wind. Winter is on its way, and the sun only rises after six o'clock now. We head out across the marsh towards Jackal Island where the zebra are congregating in their thousands. The sun breaks through and we settle down at the nearby pans to await the arrival of a group of ten elephant we see moving towards us. Soon they arrive, and drink noisily only metres from where we lie on the damp earth alongside the Land Rover, parked at the water's edge. After a while the elephant drift away and groups of zebra begin to move down, wading chest-deep into the water to drink. They are very highly strung and panic at the slightest movement, even when a sub-adult greater kestrel *(Falco rupicoloides)* swoops low overhead while chasing a small bird. Later we photograph another kestrel, or perhaps the same one, perched on a fallen tree on the track back across the marsh. In the afternoon just as we are preparing to venture out again a storm blows up and it pours with rain, eventually settling into a steady drizzle that continues all afternoon. In the early evening we find two leopards lying among the rocks on the side of Kudu Koppies, but it is too dark for photography and there is too much intervening vegetation for a flash to be effective.

4

May 4 After an early supper, we pack our bedding into *Arabella* and head out to the marsh, intending to spend the night among the zebra herds to record any predator action. However, when we arrive at the southern end of the marsh the zebra have disappeared, the tracks all heading south into the Mababe area. As we drive along the edge of the marsh we notice four lionesses and drive across to them. It's Maome's Pride, or the remnants of it as the pride has disintegrated without the leadership of the lioness, Maome, who disappeared a few months earlier in December 1994. The pride appears to be heading in the same direction as the zebra spoor, so we follow, hoping to film a zebra hunt. There are three adult lionesses and a younger one, known as the Princess, the only cub from the pride to survive to adulthood in many years.

Darkness comes quickly in this part of Africa and we have to concentrate hard not to lose the lions as they make their way through thick acacia thornbush. We stay back as far as possible, tracking them with a red-filtered spotlight so as not to interfere with their night vision — or that of any potential prey. The lions lead us a merry dance through low lying areas now swampy after all the rain, deep pot-holes that could easily swallow the Land Rover, and wall-to-wall thornbush. Eventually, at about 10 o'clock, the lions stop and rest, sleeping about 10 metres from where we stop.

After an hour the lions awaken and begin to groom each other, then rise, stretch and move off. They walk a short distance, then stop and listen intently off to the right. Then they split up and move off rapidly, slinking through the bushes like ghostly wraiths. We follow as quickly as we can and emerge into a clearing where we see a herd of impala grouped on the far side. The impala must have caught the lions' scent, for they appear very skittish and nervous. The three lionesses circle the impala, while the Princess lies alongside our vehicle, not participating in the hunt. Suddenly one lioness charges the herd and immediately pulls down a large ram. The herd scatters wildly; a ram and two ewes dash past the front of the Land Rover — straight towards the Princess. At the last moment they see her and veer wildly in front of the vehicle. The ram makes it easily, but one of the ewes, bunching her haunches to jump, leaps straight at the windscreen. I throw myself flat on the passenger seat — Sharna is standing in the roof hatch to operate the spotlight — just as the antelope smashes into the glass with a jarring thud. The windscreen shatters, and the impala slides off the Land Rover, its neck broken. The Princess, obviously excited by all the action around her, stares at the feebly kicking form for a few seconds, then darts forward and bites into the impala's throat in the typical lion stranglehold.

1

1 *Lions are the only truly social members of the cat family, spending their waking hours interacting with other members of the pride.*

2 *Hyenas are at their most active between sunset and sunrise.*

3 *An impala lamb provides little more than a dainty snack for an adult lioness.*

4 *The lionesses tear into the young impala with gusto, satisfying their gnawing hunger.*

5 *Lions possess sharp eyesight and are able to hunt prey by day and by night.*

2

3

4

5

Soon the impala is still, and the Princess lies proudly with her trophy. She licks tentatively at the carcass, then chews at a hoof. Again she licks at the impala, then looks about her, not knowing what to do with her unexpected booty. She does not appear to know how to tear the skin and open up the impala to get to the meat inside. She has most likely never had to deal with a kill before. Minutes later, the other lionesses rush up. The Princess makes a defiant attempt at protecting her 'kill', but gets a few quick and hefty cuffs to the head. The adults make short shrift of the task at hand and soon all four lions are feeding greedily. Hyenas start to gather and their whooping calls add to the night chorus as we decide to call it a night, driving a short distance away and unrolling our bedroll on the Land Rover's roofrack. Later we are woken by the nearby roaring of a male lion who has come to join the lionesses at the kill. It is one of the primeval sounds of Africa, and we listen contentedly as we drift off to sleep again.

May 6 It is soon after sunrise and still bitterly cold when we find five cheetah near Marabou Pan. It is a female with four of her offspring, now almost full-grown. They appear to have killed an impala, which has been stolen from them by several hyenas. The cheetah walk haughtily away, crossing through the belt of woodland to the western side of the marsh. We spend all day with them, watching four unsuccessful attempts at hunting more impala, then leave them about 9 o'clock when they appear to settle down for the night. Cheetah generally do not move about much after dark, except on nights when they may hunt by the light of a full moon.

May 7 We return to the cheetah before sunrise and find them where we left them last night, going about their morning ablutions. Several hyena are lying around, as well as about a dozen black-backed jackal, all waiting for the chance to steal from the cheetahs' kill. As the sun rises the cheetah begin to move across the marsh, climbing up into the branches of the many dead trees to scan the surroundings. Every now and then one of the cheetah charges at the hyena, the ruff on its neck raised to make it look bigger and more fearsome. Although the hyena stay out of range, they don't look particularly threatened. Soon though the cheetah lie down again, perhaps realising there is no point in hunting while the scavengers follow.

By about half past eight the hyena have drifted away and only two jackal remain, and the cheetah move off again. Within 15 minutes they have made two unsuccessful attempts at impala, both times the hunt being spoiled by the over-eagerness of the youngsters, who are supposed to stay behind while the mother hunts out front. The cheetah move under some trees on a slight rise and lie there panting, out of breath after two high-speed chases in quick succession. They are in a perfect vantage place covering a large grassy vlei, and we park the Land Rover in such a way that we are positioned for quick action should anything occur.

1 – 5 The impala ram jinks and swerves, but is no match for the speedy cheetah and her sub-adult cubs.

6 A perfect vantage place overlooking the surrounding vlei.

7 Cheetah take advantage of tall features like dead trees and termite mounds from which to survey the open plains.

8 Exhausted after two high-speed chases, one of the cheetah yawns wearily.

1

2

3

6

4

5

Suddenly we notice an impala ram running across the vlei, straight towards where the cheetah lie. The adult female immediately rises and slinks stealthily forward. Seconds later she charges. A cheetah can run at speeds up to 110 kilometres per hour and accelerates to that pace within a few strides. The impala does not stand a chance. Seeing the cheetah streaking at it like an Exocet missile, the ram, now only about 30 metres away, jinks and swerves in a desperate effort to evade death. The cheetah lengthens its stride and hauls it in easily. Her right paw flashes out and hooks at the impala, unbalancing it and it crashes to the earth, the spotted cat at its throat in an instant. Within seconds the four sub-adults are tearing at the flesh, their mother still with her jaws clamped tight across the impala's windpipe in a suffocating grip.

7

The cheetah feed voraciously, anxious to eat their fill before the arrival of other predators and scavengers. Already two jackal prowl the fringes of the kill, and now and then a cheetah turns to chase it off, rearing up then banging its forefeet on the ground in a threat display. One by one the cheetah are sated and fall away from the feeding frenzy, their faces bloodied and covered with gore.

8

May 9 I meet microlight pilot Grant Truthe to do some aerial photography, and we take off soon after sunrise, heading south over the marsh. We spot several herds of buffalo along the eastern side, and a number of small pockets of zebra in the candlepod acacia scrub further south, although we do not find the big groups we are looking for. In the afternoon Sharna and I drive south and find the Sethlare Pride, looking healthy and well-fed, lying alongside the waterhole at Wild Dog Vlei. They all eventually go down to the water to drink, and show only the faintest of interest when I get out of the Land Rover nearby to photograph them at ground level.

May 14 A cold wind greets us this morning and we bundle up in winter woolies before heading out to Motsibi Island where we had seen 11 wild dogs late yesterday. We find them lying on a promontory where they have a good view over the open marshlands, though they seem more intent on sleeping out of the wind than in hunting. They show brief interest when several tsessebe canter past, but do not give chase.

May 16 Shortly after sunrise we find the family of five cheetah moving along the eastern marsh road and follow as they cross the marsh. They are in high spirits and chase each other in circles, leaping and pouncing in play rituals that mimic their hunting techniques, but show no inclination to hunt, even when they see a herd of impala nearby. Later we photograph a lilac-breasted roller *(Coracias caudata)*, one of Africa's most beautiful birds, as it perches on a tree stump nearby, then we move on to the pans near Jackal Island where we see several elephants at the water but little other game.

1

2

1 *The wild dogs seem more intent on staying out of the bitter wind in the long grass, than in following their prey.*
2 *One of the world's most beautiful birds, the lilac-breasted roller is a relatively common inhabitant in many wilderness areas of Africa.*
3 *We spot several herds of buffalo from the air, feeding along the eastern side of the Savuti Marsh.*
4 *Looking healthy and well-fed, the lions drink at Wild Dog Vlei.*

Overleaf: *The cheetah show no inclination to hunt despite the nearby presence of a herd of impala.*

3

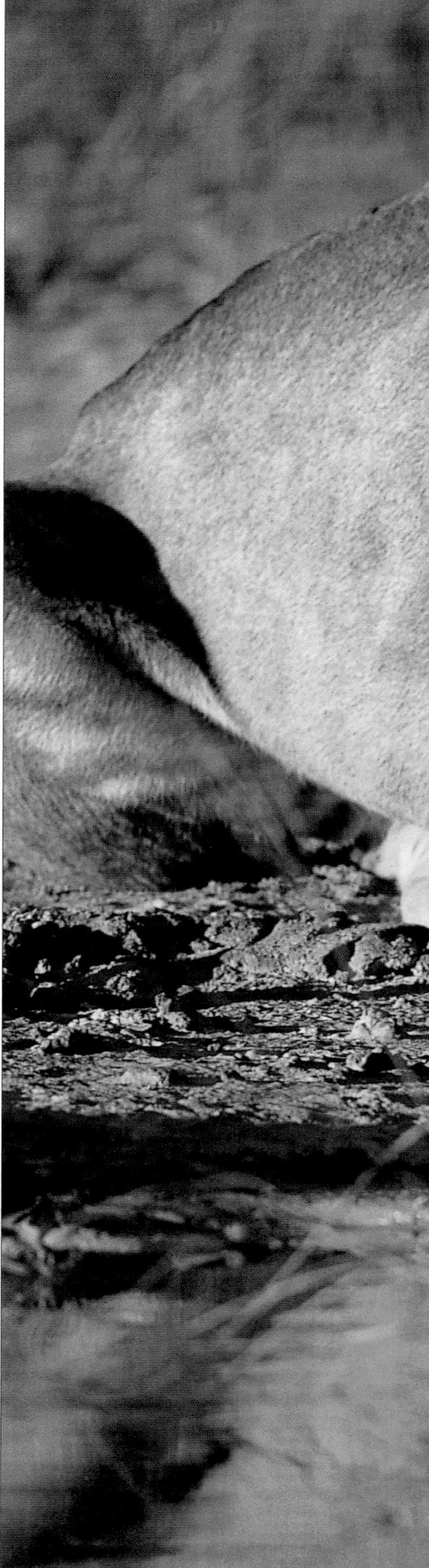

4

WINTER
A season of hardship

The bleak, cheerless mid-year months present an eternal challenge to Chobe's wildlife, which must adapt to this time of barren austerity.

Winter is a dry and harsh time in Savuti. The wind whips up towering, swirling 'dust devils' and brittle leaves fall endlessly from gaunt, withering trees. The sun-bleached grass crackles underfoot, and dust hangs choking in the midday heat. Waterholes shrivel and dry until vast herds of game clamour around the few remaining, shrinking pools. Over the aeons, Chobe's wildlife has become accustomed to these cycles of wet and dry, feast and famine, but now, because the tourist industry demands it, there are a number of permanent waterpoints in Savuti. In the past during the dry winter season the animals would migrate north to the permanent waters of the Chobe River and Linyanti Swamp, giving Savuti's vegetation respite from continual grazing pressure. Now many animals that normally would have left the area, remain all year round. Every day long lines of animals trek to the few man-made waterholes, and sometimes up to a hundred elephants will be there at any one time. After drinking their fill, they leave again and set off on the long haul back from whence they came. It is a hard time for Savuti's wildlife, alleviated only by the nutrient-rich grasses that grow here and there, and hardy acacia scrub varieties that blossom and bloom when all around is barren and bare.

Above: *During the dry winter months, brittle leaves fall endlessly from the gaunt, withering trees.* ***Left:*** *A lone elephant drinks from one of the few remaining, but steadily shrinking, rainwater pools.*

2

1 A giant eagle owl wakes us at first light, then poses for the camera.
2 & 3 We spend the morning at the rapidly drying Jackal Island Pans, photographing elephants splashing and drinking the muddy waters.
4 The impala spot the wild dogs and stand staring fixedly in their direction.

1

July 8 Savuti in winter is very different from the lush abundance after the summer rains. The countryside has dried out and where recently there was green grassland, now it is yellowed and lifeless. Dust hangs in a pall behind the vehicle and most seasonal waterholes are dry. The deep rainwater pans at Jackal Island still hold water though, and the elephants come down to drink in a steady procession throughout the day.

July 10 A giant eagle owl wakes us at first light, hooting in the tree over our tent. We stumble out into the pre-dawn cold to boil water for tea and ready ourselves for the morning's outing, watched closely by the owl, who obligingly stays put until the sun rises and poses perfectly while we set up a camera and tripod. Then we make our way to the Jackal Island Pans and spend the morning photographing elephants drinking and splashing in the water. There are now only a handful of zebra left on the marsh, stragglers left behind by the big herds that have returned to their winter feeding grounds near Linyanti, and even they seem to be moving steadily northwards.

July 15 Driving along the main road north from Savuti, we find a pack of six wild dogs trotting unconcernedly along. Generally wild dogs show little fear of man or vehicles, and these are no exception, barely glancing over their shoulders as we fall in behind them. We follow for about two kilometres before they turn off the track and head towards nearby Harvey's Pans. Hoping they may be on their way to hunt, we overtake and rush ahead, planning to see if there is any potential prey and positioning ourselves for photography. A few impala are scattered about on the open plains and we park the Land Rover diagonally across from where we estimate the dogs will appear. Soon they arrive — but one of the impala spots them immediately and snorts in alarm. The rest of the herd immediately look up, alert to danger. They stand staring transfixed for a few seconds, then take off, running and leaping across the open plain. Two dogs give chase briefly, but it is a lost cause and they rejoin the others, slinking off to lie in the shade of a mopane tree, where they remain sleeping all day.

3

4

1 A black-backed jackal laps at the waters of one of the pans near Jackal Island ...
2 ... while a lone old bull elephant drinks quietly nearby.
3 A male Burchell's sandgrouse wades belly deep to absorb water in its breast feathers. It will transport the water to nest-bound chicks as far as 60 kilometres away.
4 A group of blue wildebeest drink their fill.

2

4

3

July 19 We lie in the shade alongside *Arabella*, parked right at the waterside at Jackal Island Pans, while countless flocks of Burchell's sandgrouse (*Pterocles burchelli*) come to drink. They regard us with curiosity, but no apparent fear and occasionally one walks right up to the end of our 500 millimetre lens, peering frankly at the strange object. We notice several males gathering water in their chest and belly feathers, wading deep into the water with feathers fluffed out to do so. Sandgrouse carry water to their young in this manner, flying as much as 60 kilometres at a time. A lone old bull elephant drinks quietly nearby, standing motionless as though asleep for long periods. Though when another elephant arrives, he strides purposefully towards the intruder and they scuffle and spar for a few minutes before the newcomer gives way and moves off. A while later several other elephants arrive, and the cantankerous old bull finally has to share his waterhole!

July 20 Returning to Jackal Island Pans we find even more sandgrouse gathering at the water's edge, including the first yellowthroated sandgrouse (*Pterocles gutturalis*) we have seen here. A lanner falcon (*Falco biarmicus*) keeps making passes over the pan, sending the sandgrouse scattering in panic, but his target is a flock of small redheaded finches (*Amadina erythrocephala*) that appears at the waterside now and again. Several groups of wildebeest arrive, eventually wading chest-deep into the water to drink their fill, but every time the falcon swoops over the pan setting the sandgrouse to flight, the wildebeest are thrown into disarray and flee the water in wild panic. Eventually satisfied that their lives are not in immediate danger, the wildebeest stand snorting nearby, tossing their heads and running in crazy circles nevertheless.

July 23 After spending the early morning at the Jackal Island Pans once more, we head for Marabou Pan (which is kept topped up by solar and diesel pumping), where we find six wild dogs asleep in the shade of a raintree. We park under a shady tree ourselves and enjoy a picnic lunch, watching the passing parade at the nearby waterhole while we wait for the dogs to awaken. From time to time they rise, stretch, and move into deeper shade, only to sleep again. Eventually just after four o'clock they rise and make their way down to the water, where several elephants are busy drinking. The elephants turn and chase the dogs, who soon give up and move away into the mopane to the east. We circle around and get ahead of them and notice a large warthog boar *(Phacochoerus aethiopicus)* limping in their direction. The warthog appears to be seriously injured, unable to use one foreleg at all, and he even gets down and crawls on his knees now and then. We feel sure we will get a good kill sequence with the dogs and position ourselves for the best vantage. The dogs lie in ambush less than 20 metres from the warthog, when suddenly he sees them. He turns to flee as the dogs surge from cover, injured foot forgotten as he takes off at full speed towards the marsh, his tail erect over his back. Astonished, we can only watch in admiration as the big pig, which only moments before was a hobbling cripple, jinks and swerves and makes his escape. After a chase of some 200 metres the dogs give up and a few metres further on the warthog disappears down his burrow, a survivor to fight another day.

July 24 Two large male cheetah kill a warthog along the eastern side of the marsh, but before they even have a chance to take a bite three hyena drive them off. The hyenas rip and tear at the carcass, and soon there are 20 jackals gathered around, making sniping runs to snatch scraps that fall free. The jackals snap and snarl at each other while jockeying for position, and there appears to be a definite hierarchy among them. The hyenas have their work cut out keeping the jackals at bay, and then one jackal manages to sneak in unseen, grabs a severed foreleg and runs off with it, only to be chased by one of the hyenas. Although a jackal should be able to outrun and out-manoeuvre the larger hyena, the added burden of the leg it carries slows it, and soon it drops its booty and runs off. The hyena picks up the leg and returns to the kill with it. Still the jackals take their chances, managing to grab scraps here and there, but the hyenas devour nearly everything and most of the jackals go hungry.

1

4

2

3

1 *A wild dog keeps a wary lookout as it bathes near a drinking elephant.*
2 *The dog watches alertly as a warthog approaches.*
3 *Snapping and snarling at each other as they jockey for position at the carcass, there appears to be a definite hierarchy among the jackals.*
4 *The elephants show no inclination to share their water with the wild dogs, who soon give up and move into the mopane scrub nearby.*
5 *Cheetah rank low in the predator hierarchy.*
6 *Jackals depend on their wit and stealth for survival.*

5

6

1

3

2

1 *A pair of dwarf mongooses warm themselves in the early morning sun.*
2 *Survivors: the remaining lionesses of the once-powerful Maome's Pride now eke out an existence around the southern fringes of the Savuti Marsh.*
3 *Redbilled oxpeckers cling to the coarse hide of a grovelling warthog.*
4 *The young leopard watches with interest as we lie in the grass for some eye-level photography.*

July 28 There are still huge flocks of sandgrouse coming in to the pans at Jackal Island and we spend some time with them before moving on to Marabou Pan. At the area known as Warthog Alley we find two very co-operative warthogs, who show no concern at all when we get out of the vehicle very close to them to take some low-angle photographs, one even walking right up to us for a closer look! They are really comical, down on their knees in the dirt while they dig for roots and tubers with their tough snouts. Several redbilled oxpeckers *(Buphagus erythrorhynchus)* cling to the warthogs' flanks, feeding on ticks and other parasites.

In the evening we drive out to Gardenia Island where we find Maome's Pride asleep in the grass. We are sitting nearby, waiting for them to awaken, when we hear a bark to our left. We turn and see a pack of wild dogs with about a dozen small puppies, standing at the treeline staring at the lions. Roused by the bark, the lions jump to their feet and give chase, the dogs fleeing for their lives. Within seconds we see three of the lionesses catch a puppy each, which they kill and eat on the spot. The rest of the dogs scattered in the deepening gloom, and we are unable to find them again.

July 31 After setting off for a late afternoon drive, we find the young male leopard at Leopard Rock. He behaves very tamely and co-operates fantastically for photography, even coming to lie in the shade of the Land Rover. We stay with him until dark, and he shows almost no concern when I alight from the Land Rover and lie down in the grass with my cameras about six metres from him.

4

1

2

3

4

August 1 We leave camp as the sun slips over the eastern horizon and drive down the dry Savuti Channel towards the marsh. Following the eastern road we find six cheetah stalking two steenbok *(Raphicerus campestris)*, but they are unsuccessful when they give chase and retire to the shade of a towering leadwood tree. We watch them for over an hour, but it appears that they have settled down to wait out the midday heat and we return to camp.

After an early lunch we head back out to the cheetah and find them as they move out to hunt. Again they stalk a steenbok, this time successfully. The adult female leads the chase, followed by the five sub-adults, and though the steenbok zigzags at high speed the cheetah gain on it with every stride. Eventually the female is close enough to stretch out and hook the little antelope's legs from beneath it and it cartwheels in the grass. In a flash the cheetah is on it, only to release it as the five youngsters run up. They give chase and pull it down again, and this time all five pile in and start tearing the small buck to pieces. The female pushes her way into the melee and all six cheetah feed voraciously, although the meal does not go far among them all. Later they chase another steenbok, but it runs like the wind and evades capture. We stay with the cheetah until after sunset, then find the Sethlare Pride drinking at Rhino Vlei as we make our way back to camp.

August 4 It is a bitterly cold morning when we leave camp shortly after sunrise, heading down the channel towards the marsh. Everywhere we see birds and animals standing warming themselves in the sun, and shortly after President's Camp we spot a leopard sunning himself in a tree. We spend most of the morning with him, and after a while he comes down out of the tree and finds a corner in the channel bed where he can lie sheltered from the cold wind. The leopard seems quite unconcerned by our proximity or the arrival of a Land Rover belonging to Okavango Wilderness Safaris. Later we move to the marsh, where we photograph a pair of courting steenbok. The little ram walks stiff-legged behind the female, prodding at her nether regions with a straight foreleg from time to time, but the doe shows scant interest in her amorous suitor and eventually he gives up and starts feeding nearby.

8

5

6

7

1-3 The steenbok has no chance against the swift cheetah.
4 All five cheetah pile in.
5 A steenbok ram prods stiff-legged at his female companion.
6 Cheetah ususally appear haughty and aloof.
7 The cheetah strike a perfect pose on a termite mound.
8 The cheetah watches intently as we approach her brood.

2

3

4

August 6 Sunrise is earlier than desired and a bitingly cold wind whistles through the flimsy canvas walls of our tent. Sharna has a slight eye infection, probably caused by the wind and dust at this time of year, and uses this as an excuse to snuggle deeper into the bed, but I drag myself out into the cold and decide to drive down the dry channel in search of the leopard we saw two days ago. In this cold, there's a good chance I'll find him sunning himself somewhere again. Soon I am near President's Camp, and I search the leeward side of the channel carefully. There! The leopard is lying in the sun, sheltered from the wind by a clump of grass, diligently preening himself. I carefully position the Land Rover nearby, set up the cameras and proceed to take photographs of him in all his glory. Suddenly the leopard looks up and tenses in the grass staring diagonally past me, towards the opposite bank of the channel. I turn and see a large herd of impala making their way down into the channel, and at the same moment the leopard flattens itself in the grass **(1)**, rolls over to his left and within seconds has melted into the undergrowth. Meanwhile the impala, oblivious to the threat, move into the open grass and begin gazing contentedly. The herd comprises at least 30 animals — a few rams, a number of ewes and at least a dozen yearlings from the previous summer. For more than an hour I sit waiting in anticipation. The impala move to and fro as they graze the short, sweet grass in the channel bed, sometimes within metres of where I assume the leopard may be, other times as much as 40 or 50 metres away. Suddenly, I see the leopard, sitting in a clump of wild sagebrush. The impala had been feeding less than 10 metres from its position, but now are some distance away. Then, for some inexplicable reason, the impala rams turn their brood back, and the herd feeds towards the leopard's position. The lead impala ram is feeding 20 metres away, 15 metres, 14, 12... Keeping my lens trained on the leopard I watch as its muscles flex under his spotted coat, then it inches forward.

1

Suddenly the impala snorts and stands transfixed, staring straight at the leopard only 10 metres from it. The big cat freezes, one paw poised in mid-air, and moves not a whisker for a full five minutes. I barely breathe until the impala relaxes, obviously satisfied that what it saw posed no threat, lowers its head and resumes feeding.

In a blur of golden action the leopard launches itself at the impala. Instantly the impala leaps back and sideways but the flying cat barely touches the ground before it is in the air again, crashing into its prey several feet above the ground **(2)**. The two twist in mid-air, the leopard with its claws locked deep into the flailing antelope's flanks **(3)**, and they crash to the ground, rolling several times as the impala fights for its life. Almost before it begins, it is over. The leopard fastens its jaws in a stranglehold over the impala's muzzle **(4)**, his forelegs clamped tight around the buck's neck **(5)** and hind legs curled underneath, ready to rip at the impala's underbelly should it continue to resist. But for the impala, the fight is over.

Quickly I drive closer to the action. The leopard barely flickers its eyes in my direction as it continues to suffocate its victim silently, crucial to avoid attracting hyenas and other hungry predators. But the impala herd gather nearby, barking their alarm and kicking up a commotion and I'm certain it will not be long before the scavengers arrive. Still the leopard and impala lie in the death clinch, though now I see the impala's eyes beginning to glaze. It takes all of 15 minutes for the impala to die, and eventually the exhausted leopard is

5

6

7

able to rise, shake himself off and examine his prize. The ram is considerably larger in body than the young leopard, and I'm puzzled by his choice, for he had had considerable opportunity to take a smaller yearling or doe.

Now the leopard begins the task of dragging his victim to safety **(6)**. Leopard are quite capable of climbing trees with prey as heavy as themselves, but I soon see that he may have bitten off more than he can chew. He struggles with the deadweight of the impala, battling to make headway up the steeply sloping sides and loose earth of the channel wall. Then I look down the channel and see a hyena approaching. The leopard sees it at the same time, and immediately flattens himself in the grass and sagebrush.

The hyena walks straight to the impala carcass and as it takes a tentative bite, the leopard launches himself at the much larger scavenger, hissing and snarling in fury **(7)**. The two predators snap and growl at each other, but the hyena has little difficulty in maintaining its position with the kill. After a while the leopard succeeds in driving the hyena away temporarily, and once more the cat makes a valiant attempt to drag its prize towards the top of the channel bank, and the beckoning trees. It is a futile effort though, and I see the hyena about to make a renewed attempt at taking the prize.

Then the most incredible thing happens. The leopard looks first at the Land Rover, then at the hyena and back to the Land Rover. Deciding the vehicle is perhaps the lesser of two evils, the big cat grabs hold of the impala, and drags it straight down towards the vehicle, not stopping until the carcass lies in the shade directly under the passenger-side door. The hyena stops in its tracks then retires to the shade of a nearby bush to ponder this new development. The leopard meanwhile sits watching in satisfaction, turns and looks straight into my eyes, gives a brief snarl, baring his fearsome fangs, and commences his meal.

I sit dumbfounded for a few minutes, then cautiously poke a camera over the doorsill and resume my photography. The leopard is feeding contentedly, less than a metre below me. Now and then he raises his eyes and stares straight into mine, baring his fangs in what I like to believe is a smile of gratitude **(8)**. He has seen the Land Rover often enough in the past to realise it presents no threat, but now the leopard has taken the process a step further and seems to regard it as some sort of ally. I feel a sense of elation, knowing I have captured the kill on film, but also in the realisation that there is a bond of trust between me and this beautiful wild animal. It is a humbling and gratifying experience.

8

CHOBE

A vista of untamed grandeur

Like the Okavango River further to the west, the Chobe flows like a river of life across the parched Kalahari sandveld and featureless mopane woodland.

Chobe is synonymous with big game, and in particular elephants, for here along the riverfront you will find one of Africa's largest remaining elephant populations. The most recent estimates reckon on 79 000 of these behemoths in Botswana, and apart from a population of about 700 in the Tuli Block Game Reserve along the eastern border with South Africa, the majority of the elephants spend part or all of the year in the Chobe environs. While the Chobe National Park encompasses a vast and diverse domain, the different regions of north-eastern Botswana are as disparate as the well-watered Okavango Delta is from the arid Central Kalahari.

The Chobe River is undoubtedly one of the most beautiful and unspoiled rivers of Africa, and to many visitors the riverfront between the village of Kasane and the public campsite at Serondella, teeming with elephant and buffalo in their hundreds and thousands, is one of the most memorable vistas in the natural world, while the remote eastern and western corners of the park distil the true essence of unspoiled wilderness.

Above: *An elephant family group drinks from the Chobe River below Serondella campsite.* ***Left:*** *The sun sets in a blaze of fiery colour over Zibadianja Lagoon in the western corner of the Chobe ecosystem.*

1

2

4

3

1 *A flock of guineafowl scratch for supper in the dust.*
2 *One of the classic views of Chobe: elephants drinking below the Karozike viewsite.*
3 *We attract a curious audience of baboons and their young while setting up camp.*
4 *The Chobe riverfront is the only place in southern Africa where the puku occurs.*

August 8 The road from Savuti northwards to the Chobe River at Kasane is long, dusty and arduous. The sand lies deep and soft in the tracks and we grind along in low gear for much of the way. Although the journey is only about 170 kilometres, the distance is measured in hours rather than kilometres and though it can be done in less, it is generally accepted to be a four to five hour trip. After setting off from Savuti early we reach Kasane in time for lunch and an ice cold drink at the spectacular Cresta Mowana Safari Lodge, situated on the river a short way out of town. As with many smaller towns and villages in Africa, the stores close for the midday lunch break and we while away the heat of the day at the Mowana before heading back into town to shop for fresh provisions. Then we make our way along the river into the park, and set up our small 'fly camp' under a spreading shade tree at Serondella. We attract an audience of baboons *(Papio ursinus)* and vervet monkeys *(Cercopithecus aethiops)*, who look for any opportunity to pilfer unattended edibles. Thanks to careless visitors over the years who have fed these animals, the baboons have now become serious pests in the public campsite as they have even learned to raid tents and will break into an unattended vehicle. Our camp now organised — with all food and edibles in locked steel trunks — we drive down to the Chobe waterfront to watch the sunset while a flock of guineafowl scratch for supper in the dirt.

August 9 A herd of elephants trumpet and carry-on in the bush around camp all night, but move off by first light and we don't see them. We awaken instead to an almighty row among the baboons in camp, screaming, barking and chasing each other up and down the trees with much baring of teeth and fangs. Later we drive along the river and photograph some puku antelope *(Kobus vardonii)* at the aptly named Puku Flats. The Chobe riverfront is reputed to be the only place in southern Africa where these antelope, close relatives of the red lechwe *(Kobus leche)* and waterbuck *(Kobus ellipsiprymnus)*, occur. We park on the bank of the sluggishly flowing river for morning tea and are entertained by a pair of spotted-necked otters *(Lutra maculicollis)* who hunt among the reeds and lily pads at the water's edge.

1

3

4

2

August 12 A beautiful pink sunrise on the riverfront heralds a huge herd of buffalo making their way off the floodplain into the thick bush away from the river. Chobe is noted for its buffalo herds, and it is an unforgettable sight to see countless hundreds of them, dust swirling overhead, moving slowly over the floodplain. Later we are fortunate to see a herd of about 30 sable antelope *(Hippotragus niger)* as they move out of the woodlands to drink at the river on Watercart Loop. The handsome black antelope with swept-back, scimitar horns are very skittish at first, but we take our time and make a slow, patient approach. The sable settle down enough to allow us within 100 metres and we expend several rolls of film on these magnificent creatures.

August 14 We leave camp before first light in an attempt to find some lions that have been roaring through the early hours of the morning, and soon find their spoor heading down the road. We track them for several kilometres before the spoor disappears into thick thornscrub west of Serondella. We return to the river, where we photograph a saddlebilled stork *(Ephippiorhynchus senegalensis)* feeding up and down in a small, muddy pool as well as a great white egret *(Egretta alba)* spearing a small 'squeaker' catfish right in front of us.

We visit Kasane for the luxury of another hotel lunch and then return to Serondella, where we find the baboons up to mischief in the campsite as usual. We have learned the only way to prevent them damaging the tent is to collapse it every morning, re-erecting it only at night when we return to camp. In the evening the elephants come down to the river as usual, and we watch the antics of several young calves cavorting along the river bank.

5

August 15 There is not much game about this morning, though once again we see very fresh lion spoor in the road. Near the luxurious Chobe Game Lodge we see a honey badger *(Mellivora capensis)* busily foraging across the grassy plains, but it is very shy and we cannot get close enough for photography. We find a troop of baboons sunning themselves at the roadside and spend an amusing hour or so with them. They are very human in their behaviour and postures, and are exceedingly entertaining when not being destructive around the camp! Later, as the day warms up more game moves down to the riverside and we see the sable antelope again, as well as another group of puku.

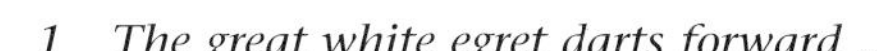

6

1 *The great white egret darts forward ...*
2 *... and spears a small squeaker catfish, which wriggles furiously in its bill.*
3 *The egret dips the struggling fish in the water ...*
4 *... and deftly manipulates it in its bill to flatten the dangerous spines in its pectoral region ...*
5 *... before swallowing its victim whole.*
6 *A herd of Cape buffalo make their way off the floodplain at sunrise.*

1

CHOBE'S FORGOTTEN EASTERN CORNER

The Nogatsaa and Tchinga region of the park, about 60 kilometres due south of Serondella, is possibly the most under-utilised section because there is no accommodation, only campsites, and in the wet season some of the roads are transformed into a treacherous quagmire. The time to visit, however, is during the dry season when several of the larger pans are artificially maintained and hold water well into the winter months, attracting huge concentrations of game. The road south from Serondella is a dusty, sandy track and at first the going is tough and requires four-wheel-drive for much of the way. At Nogatsaa the bungalows of the old camp are in ruins, but there is a public campsite at Tchinga. Although the roads are in reasonably good repair, the intersections are unmarked, although concrete bollards at each turning indicate that once-upon-a-time the situation may have been much better. We find it sad that in spite of the high park fees charged to visitors, basic maintenance appears to be neglected, a malaise evident throughout the park.

August 18 We arrive at Tchinga to find there are no facilities for campers, although the site is marked on park maps as a public camping site. There is, however, a solar-powered pump to supply water to a nearby waterhole, and we find that we are able to draw fresh, clean water from a tap at the pumphouse. We set up our tent in solitary splendour in a cluster of tall mopane trees where we have a good outlook over the waterhole, and spend the remainder of the afternoon undertaking repairs to the Land Rover's clutch mechanism and watching the passing parade. Apart from numerous elephants, the waterhole was also visited by several greater kudu, giraffe and warthog.

2

3

1 *The coqui francolin is shy and retiring.*
2 *An elephant skull perfectly framed by mopane leaves ...*
3 *Roan antelope are both rare and endangered as a species.*
4 *Several giraffe visit the waterhole.*
5 *A herd of sable antelope moves off into the woodland.*

4

5

1

2

3

1 *We see several elephants in the colourful mopane scrub.*
2 *Kudu are common throughout the Tchinga area.*
3 *The mopane woodland is resplendent in its 'winter plumage'.*
4 *A hyena drinks from one of the man-made waterholes in the region.*

August 19 Two lions had a roaring duel near camp in the early hours of the morning, a crescendo of primordial reverberation that almost has the tent walls quivering! What a magnificent sound, one that always gives us a thrill despite our many years in the bush, something we hope we'll never tire of hearing. We rise as soon as it is light enough to see and drive around the area looking for them, but once again the lions elude us. The mopane woodland, the predominant vegetation here, is resplendent in its winter 'plumage', a palette of orange, brown, gold and yellow. Everywhere we drive we see elephant, as well as several groups of zebra and a number of giraffe, though we find that the game here, off the beaten track, is unfamiliar with vehicles and difficult to approach and photograph.

4

August 21 Once again we hear lions roaring throughout the night, but fail to find them in the morning. Leaving camp just after sunrise we witness a herd of sable antelope moving away from the waterhole where they must have been drinking before first light. We follow them for some distance and when they move into thick mopane scrub we go after them on foot, but they spot us and gallop away. Later we photograph two magnificent kudu bulls, then return to camp for lunch and to repair a punctured tyre. We spend the afternoon at the Tchinga waterhole, watching the elephants as they come to drink and bathe. Incredibly, we see one elephant with six tusks, although they are small and under-developed. Unfortunately it is too dark for photography, and the elephant does not come within flash range.

August 24 The August winds have arrived with a vengeance, late but in full spate. We spend the morning making sure our tent is well secured and drive in a few extra pegs before setting off, the Land Rover buffeted by the gusting wind that sends dust and leaves swirling everywhere. Many of the animals, too, seem to be perturbed by the wind, and although we drive for several hours we see little other than a lone steenbok, a few warthogs and a herd of impala.

August 25 We leave camp early and drive to the site of the old Ngwezumba Dam. Although there are still a few pools that hold water from the rains earlier in the year, we see little sign of game other than elephants, spotting several in beautifully coloured mopane. We follow a track to the south-east and come to another waterhole with a solar pump station, Poha Pan, where we encounter a herd of impala and see the pug marks left by a big male lion in the mud at the water's edge. From here we follow another track and turn north-east, making our way back towards Tchinga. We pass through a magnificent mopane forest, the trees tall and straight and in spectacular colour, and are lucky to find two elephants in amongst them. We alight from the Land Rover and follow the elephants on foot to photograph them in the splendid setting, then find an old elephant skull lying perfectly framed by mopane leaves (p. 64). Later we manage to photograph a few coqui francolin *(Francolinus coqui)*, generally shyer than the more common redbilled and Swainson's francolins.

4

1

August 28 The weather has been overcast and chilly for the past two days, and although we have covered a great deal of countryside we have still been unsuccessful in our search for the roan antelope reputed to occur in these parts, although we do see their close relatives, the sable, fairly regularly. Driving through the mopane woodland we see four big old buffalo bulls, 'daga boys' as the hunters call them for the thick mud or 'daga' that typically coats their hide after wallowing. The buffalo appear to be very nervous and run off into the bush as we approach, often a sign that there has been some hunting activity in the surrounding area. This part of the park is close to the eastern boundary, where a hunting outfitter operates a shooting concession, which could account for the shyness of much of the game here.

2

1 *Warthog sexes can be told apart by the number of 'warts' on their faces, one on either side in the females and two in the males, as seen here.*
2 *An old buffalo bull peers warily at us, while a yellowbilled oxpecker scours his legs for ticks.*
3 *The old Ngwezumba Dam still holds a few pools of water late in the dry season.*
4 *An elephant strides through the tall, mature mopane forest.*
5 *A hyena's jaws are more powerful than a lion's.*

3

5

August 29 After an early drive through the mopane forest we return to camp and pack for the return trip to Kasane, where we restock our provision trunk and purchase fuel before heading back into the park. We stop at Serondella to use the shower facilities, then continue our journey, for we are heading to Linyanti and the Selinda Concession far to the west.

SWAMPS AND SPILLWAYS

The Linyanti and Selinda regions in the north-western corner of the park are also not as well-frequented as the main Chobe River section. In contrast to the dryness of Savuti and the eastern sections, Linyanti shares many similarities with the Okavango Delta and is well-watered throughout much of the year. This is the dry season range of much of Chobe's wildlife, and large breeding herds of elephant are in particular prominence. The abundance of elephants in the region is noticeable in the havoc portrayed in the woodlands. Here countless trees lie toppled and dying where these huge pachyderms have passed. Although many people decry this 'habitat destruction' by elephants we reflect on the fact that this is a role nature intended for elephants, and perhaps we are merely seeing a natural modification of the environment which, while making it unsuitable for certain species, opens it up for others. Nature is in a state of continuous flux and we wonder what would have been said had elephants killed all the trees on the Savuti Marsh, rather than a wet cycle that drowned their roots. Perhaps those with an interventionist philosophy would consider damming the upper reaches of the Savuti Channel to prevent a recurrence!

August 30 The track to Linyanti from Savuti is one of the worst in Botswana and we are relieved when we see the change in vegetation marking the edge of the Linyanti Swamp appearing ahead of us. Arriving at the tree line marking the beginning of the riverine forest, we turn west and shortly thereafter reach the Department of Wildlife and National Parks offices, where we announce our arrival to the officer in charge before heading for the nearby campsite. We choose a site looking out over reed and papyrus beds beneath a towering leadwood tree *(Combretum imberbe)* that offers good shade throughout the day. Later we explore the area, although the Chobe National Park has only a seven kilometre stretch of river frontage here, seeing several family groups of elephant as well as zebra, kudu, waterbuck and giraffe.

3

4

2

1 *The Linyanti region shares many similarities with the Okavango Delta further to the west.*

2 *A male waterbuck shows the distinctive white ring which encircles its rump.*

3 *Cape turtle doves drink at the water's edge.*

4 *The Linyanti swamp is home to countless huge crocodiles.*

5 *Fish eagles are a common sight along the waterways.*

September 1

We leave camp early, having heard lions calling shortly before sunrise, and find their spoor in the road nearby. We follow the tracks down towards the river and soon come across a group of three lionesses with some small cubs. At first the cubs are very curious, peering inquisitively at our vehicle, but then tire of the game and crawl under a dense bush to sleep. We leave them and continue on our way, encountering a small herd of roan antelope in the mopane woodland several kilometres away from the river. Roan are naturally very skittish animals and are rarely seen in the Chobe National Park so we consider ourselves fortunate when we manage to get a few photographs of them before they disappear into the bush.

Linyanti lies on Botswana's northern border with Namibia, and has experienced a considerable amount of poaching from across the border in the past. A strong Botswana Defence Force presence in the area today has put a check on illegal hunting, but the elephants in particular appear to be under severe stress and are noticeably aggressive. There are several accounts by local safari guides of elephants making serious charges and tusking vehicles in this region, and we take extra care when photographing these normally placid creatures.

1

2

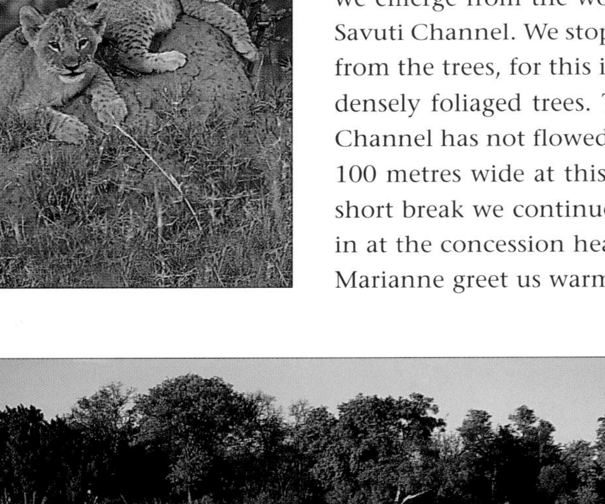

September 4

Breaking camp early, we set off for Selinda further to the west, heading first away from the river before turning to follow a winding track through magnificent mopane country. Once again we see several roan antelope, as well as numerous zebra and the ubiquitous elephants. Selinda is a private concession area lying to the west of the upper reaches of the Savuti Channel and the large Zibadianja Lagoon from whence the channel flows. A hunting territory until recently, it is now controlled by Kasane-based Linyanti Explorations, who have established two comfortable tented photographic safari camps in the area, with plans for another further west in the future. They also run the popular Chobe Chilwero camp near Kasane.

The journey goes well, and after negotiating a very sandy final 13-kilometre stretch we emerge from the woodland on to a bridge made from mopane logs, straddling the Savuti Channel. We stop in the middle of the bridge, relieved to be out in the open away from the trees, for this is tsetse fly country and the little biters occur wherever there are densely foliaged trees. There is but a trickle of water under the bridge, for the Savuti Channel has not flowed since 1981, but we admire the dry channel bed, which must be 100 metres wide at this point, and wonder if it will flow again in our lifetime. After a short break we continue on our way and soon reach our intended campsite. We check in at the concession headquarters nearby, where manager Andre Maartens and his wife Marianne greet us warmly.

3

4

1 *Lionesses typically have litters of one to three cubs.*
2 *The lion cubs peer inquisitively at us.*
3 *We emerge from the woodland on to a sturdy bridge made of mopane poles.*
4 *The sun sets in a spectacular red ball behind a stand of vegetable ivory palms and a small herd of impala.*

1

September 5 It is unseasonally overcast when we wake up, and a cold wind makes the morning unpleasant. We drive to the headwaters of the Savuti Channel where there is a large pool occupied by at least 50 hippo, but the light is too gloomy for photography. We explore further down the channel where we have several favourite pools remembered from previous years, but now they are all bone dry and the countryside barren of life. We backtrack and come across a large pack of wild dogs near the camp where film-makers Dereck and Beverly Joubert have their base. The dogs show scant concern when we make a close approach, but seem to be very interested in something they can smell on the ground, and rush around sniffing at everything. Looking closely we see the spoor of several lions and deduce that this is what has upset the dogs, for the predators are deadly enemies.

Driving around the area, which we last visited while still a hunting concession, it is noticeable how much more relaxed and approachable the game has become since the cessation of hunting activities. We reflect on the relative merits of benign (non-consumptive) and consumptive utilisation of natural resources. In the days when this was a hunting concession, a big male lion could earn income once in his life, and make one hunter happy. Today the same lion is a perpetual attraction, and can satisfy innumerable eco-tourists.

2

3

September 6 An elephant keeps us awake for much of the night, pushing down trees uncomfortably close to where we have erected our tent, trumpeting furiously whenever another elephant encroaches on his territory, and generally just being noisy. He is so close we hear every mouthful being chewed, and the ripping and shredding as he tears leaves and branches overhead. His stomach rumbles are so loud they sound like a train passing nearby. When we rise at first light he has moved some distance away, but from his footprints in the loose soil around camp we see that he passed within two metres of our flimsy nylon tent several times, and a pile of steaming dung lies right alongside. We drive north towards the Selinda Camp area, passing two honey badgers who disappear down a hole as we approach, then stopping to photograph a group of greater kudu bulls. Later we see a bull giraffe with at least 20 yellowbilled oxpeckers *(Buphagus africanus)* clustered on his neck and flanks, but frustratingly most of the birds remain on the far (shaded) side of his body when we try to photograph them. We find a redbilled francolin feeding on the pale yellow blossoms in a candlepod acacia bush, looking for all the world as though it is surrounded by snowflakes.

Later we find 14 spotted hyena lying scattered in the long grass and sagebrush. One of them chews incessantly on an old, weathered piece of hippo hide, defending it vigorously whenever one of the others approaches. The sun sets in a spectacular ball of fire, enhanced by the heavy haze that hangs in the western sky after the raging wind of the past few days has stirred up clouds of dust.

4

5

1 *A redbilled francolin feeds amid the blossoms of a candlepod acacia.*
2 *The honey badger runs towards its burrow.*
3 *At least 20 yellowbilled oxpeckers clamber over this bull giraffe's neck and flanks.*
4 *The wild dogs show scant concern as we approach.*
5 *A baboon watches us intently from his perch.*

September 8 Making our way to the hippo pool just after sunrise, we find several hippo still out of the water after their night's wanderings. Hippo will walk as much as 30 kilometres from water at night to find suitable grazing, and with the dry conditions prevailing at present we estimate these hippos must be travelling far to find food, for they appear to be exhausted when they return to the water each morning. Although the hippo generally sleep peacefully for much of the day, now and then one will raise its head and bellow forth, setting off a chain reaction among the others in the pod, not unlike different instruments of an orchestra striking up and entering the chorus. From time to time there are territorial clashes among the males in the pool, with much gnashing of teeth and loud grunting and bellowing.

Large numbers of redbilled and yellowbilled oxpeckers flit around, alighting on one hippo for a quick feed before moving to the next. When they find an open wound on a hippo's back they worry at it until the hippo, annoyed at the pestering, chases them off with a flick of the tail, accurately targeting a squirt of water at the offending bird. A lone African jacana *(Actophilornis africanus)* trots about the water's edge searching for tidbits, then darts across to land on a hippo's back, strolling about from one hippo to another as though this were the most natural thing in the world.

September 9 After a quick visit to the hippo pool we retire to the floodplain in front of our camp to photograph the red lechwe that graze there, but they seem unsettled and move into the dense reedbeds when we approach. We return to camp early and

1

1 Both red- and yellowbilled oxpeckers alight on the hippo's back for a quick feed.

2 A lone African jacana, or lilytrotter, strolls across the hippo's back.

3 Hippo cows are highly protective of their small calves and usually move away from the main herd.

4 Water flies in every direction as a hippo makes a late and hurried return to the pool after its nocturnal ramblings.

2

3

4

watch the baboons feeding in the jackalberry trees *(Diospyros mespiliformis)* all around. The trees are in fruit at present, and attract baboons, vervet monkeys and a host of fruit-eating birds such as green pigeons *(Treron calva)*, Meyer's parrots *(Poicephalus meyeri)* and grey louries *(Corythaixoides concolor)*. The baboons here have not become habituated to people and do not present any camp-raiding problems, nevertheless we do not leave anything edible where they might find it, thus associating our camp with food.

1

September 11 While lying at the edge of the hippo pool to obtain water-level photographs a Cape clawless otter *(Aonyx capensis)* and her solitary young come waddling across the grassy floodplain towards us. Unfortunately the sun is directly behind them, making photography difficult, and when we try to move our position slightly they see us and change direction, soon disappearing into a reed-filled pool. When we depart to return to camp we see a large herd of roan antelope that have come down to drink at a nearby pool, but they flee as soon as they see the Land Rover.

Later in the day we spend time at Zibadianja Lagoon, rueing the fact that it is filled with hippo and crocodile, for the sparkling blue water looks exceedingly inviting in the afternoon heat. Several elephants are feeding in the reedbeds, and we see a lone reedbuck *(Redunca arindum)* on a small palm island near the lagoon. The towering vegetable ivory palms *(Hyphaene petersiana)* are a striking feature of the landscape in Selinda, enhancing the impressions of a tropical wildlife paradise. Here and there we notice a large cluster of wild tree orchids which grow halfway up a palm's smooth, vertical trunk.

Towards sunset we find one of the guides from Selinda Camp sitting with his guests near a lone cheetah, and he shows us where we can find a lioness and her three cubs. The lioness has apparently appropriated the cheetah's impala kill and her offspring are feeding on it with gusto. We remain with the lions until after 9 o'clock, photographing the cubs as they clamber over their mother to suckle before falling asleep. A night drive in search of nocturnal creatures reveals numerous hippo feeding on the floodplains, a lone serval *(Felis serval)*, countless springhares *(Pedetes capensis)* and a very wary Selous mongoose *(Paracynictis selousi)*, but all prove unco-operative and difficult to photograph.

3

2

1 *A lone reedbuck stares out from the undergrowth on one of the small palm islands.*
2 *Dwarfed by the towering palms, the giraffe is unlikely even to be able to reach the wild tree orchids growing halfway up the trunk.*
3 *The Cape clawless otter turns and scampers nervously away from us, disappearing into a nearby pool.*
4 *A female black-backed jackal picks up one of her pups to move it to a safer den.*

4

September 12 We return to the lions at sunrise to find the cubs busily chewing at the remains of the carcass between bouts of tug o' war over various bits and pieces. While they play, we observe the cubs mimic behaviour and skills they will one day use in hunting and killing prey as adults. One of the cubs actually clamps its tiny jaws over the muzzle of the long-dead impala in imitation of the suffocation hold we have seen often in real kills. From time to time the lioness rises and scoops sand over the bloody stain and scattered entrails, obviously in an effort to mask the scent of death from scavengers and other predators. She refuses to allow her cubs to suckle, encouraging them rather to feed on the meat she has brought them, and later when she herself starts eating the cubs wander off through the palm scrub. Unable to follow through the thickets, we drive around to the other side of the small palm island and see the cubs clambering in the branches of a toppled African mangosteen tree *(Garcinia livingstonei)*. Missing her cubs, the lioness soon begins the low, muted 'come to me' grunt-call and her three youngsters go bounding back to her. She leads them away from the remains of the carcass and settles down in the shade of a small thorny shrub, where she allows the cubs to suckle from her before they all fall asleep. We remain with the lions for the rest of the day, but apart from moving with the shade as the sun arcs across the sky, they provide no further entertainment and we return to camp at nightfall.

1

2

1 *One of the cubs peers out from behind the safety of mother's back.*
2 *A cub rubs its back under its mother's jaw, just one of many social bonding activities the cats perform.*
3 *The lioness allows her offspring to suckle from her before they all fall asleep in the shade.*
4 *We find the cubs clambering around the branches of a fallen tree.*

3

4

1

September 14 The palm islands in the area — high ground that become true islands in years of heavy rain and high waters — are striking features of the landscape. The dominant vegetation is a combination of both wild date palms *(Phoenix reclinata)* and vegetable ivory palms *(Hyphaene petersiana)*. The islands, like most of the smaller islands in the Okavango Delta and indeed throughout this generally flat landscape, usually originate as termite mounds. The termite activity both raises areas of land above the surrounding flatness and enriches the soil, encouraging the growth of trees and other vegetation. As the termitaria expand, their bases join together, thus forming larger islands, adding to the diversity of habitats of the region. We spend the morning exploring several of these attractive palm clusters, and although we see little game we find evidence that the palms are heavily utilised as feed by elephants.

In the evening we visit the hippo pool at the top of the Savuti Channel, but the hippos are disappointingly inactive. Later, as the sun dips below the western horizon, several breeding herds of elephants emerge from the nearby treeline and make their way to the water. We count over 100 of these grey giants, the adult cows fussing over their youngsters who splash and frolic with abandon in the muddy waters. A heavy cloud of dust hangs over the scene and we watch amused as the hippos demonstrate their displeasure at the invasion of their pool. From time to time a hippo moves closer to where the elephants bathe, then rolls over on to its back, its jaws agape and displaying its fearsome teeth to the intruders. The elephants ignore the display, though occasionally one of the young males rushes at a hippo that has come too close, flicking out with its trunk, flaring its ears and bellowing a sharp, shrill scream of annoyance.

4

2

3

1 *From time to time one of the hippos approaches the elephants, rolling on to its back in a display we do not fully understand.*
2 *The elephants emerge from the treeline and make their way to the water.*
3 *Oxpeckers cluster on the back of a hippopotamus, feeding on parasites but also worrying at scratches and wounds sustained in its activities in and out of water.*
4 *We explore the palm clusters by Land Rover, finding a young boabab tree.*

1

2

September 18 The past few days have been windy and overcast with very little game about, so we have begun to spend more time in search of nocturnal creatures. As usual we see countless hippo out grazing on the short grasses of the floodplains, then the beam of the spotlight picks out an unusual shape loping through the grass. It's an aardwolf *(Proteles cristatus)*, a harmless insect-eating mammal that specialises in feeding on termites. We drive closer and the aardwolf stops and stares curiously at us, before turning and ambling off again. I alight from the vehicle and follow on foot with a camera while Sharna keeps the red-filtered spotlight on the dainty jackal-like animal. As I approach the aardwolf turns to face me, erecting its long mane of upper body hair in a ploy ostensibly to increase its apparent size and frighten off potential predators. But after a few moments of uncertainty, the aardwolf appears to decide I pose no threat, and returns to foraging for insects in the grass. Later the aardwolf lies down to rest, again appearing to be unconcerned by my proximity, and I am able to photograph at will.

Leaving the aardwolf, we head back towards our camp and see two Cape porcupines *(Hystrix africaeaustralis)* near the Zibadianja safari lodge. Again I leave the vehicle and follow on foot, but these huge rodents are not prepared to co-operate and I only manage a few shots before they scurry away into the night. We spot a honey badger and again I leave the Land Rover and approach on foot. The badger turns and charges at me, snarling aggressively, and I beat a hasty retreat. Honey badgers are reputed to be among the bravest and most ferocious of all animals, willing to take on even lions and buffalo in defence of their territory, and have a reputation for attacking the scrotum!

3

1 *We find two porcupines foraging across the floodplains.*
2 *At night hippo wander considerable distances from water in search of forage.*
3 *The windy conditions cause a heavy haze in the sky, which results in spectacular red sunsets.*
4 *The beam of the spotlight picks out an unusual shape loping through the grass... an aardwolf.*

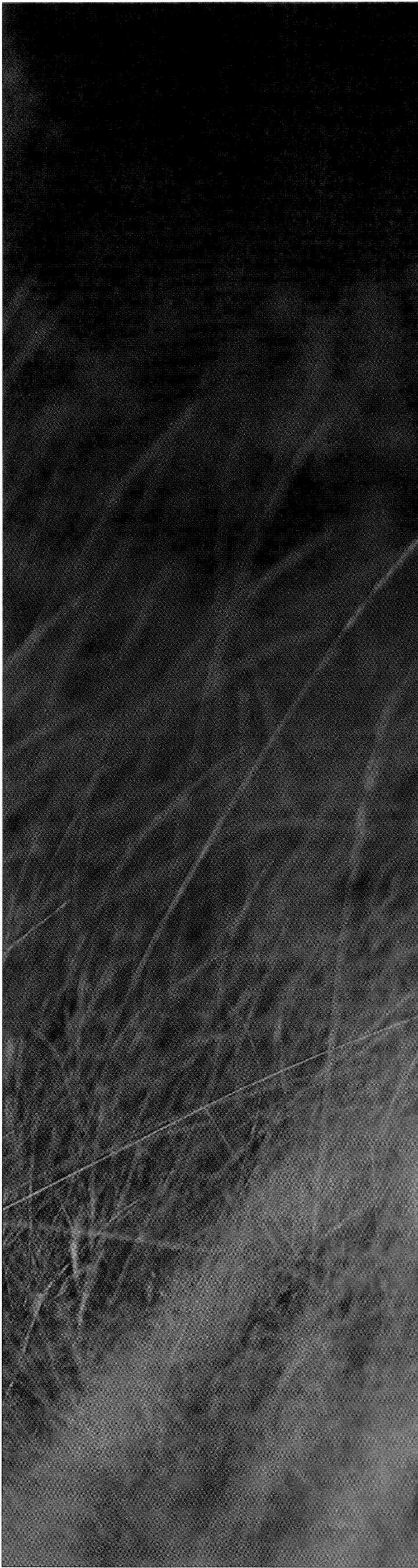

4

September 21 Despite a bitterly cold wind this morning, with dust swirling everywhere, we head north across the floodplains in search of the Selinda lion pride, which we could hear calling throughout the night. We drive from one palm island to another without success and are about to give up the search when we find them, lying screened from the wind in the lee of a small grassy knoll. There are 22 in the pride, 8 lionesses and 14 cubs ranging in age from a few months to about a year-and-a-half. The lioness with her three small cubs has rejoined the pride now, and the older cubs delight in playing with the little ones in rough and tumble games. From time to time the small cubs tire of the robust play, retreating to where their mother lies, mewing for her attention and attempting to suckle from her swollen teats. Reluctantly, she rolls on to her back and the youngsters drink greedily from her, squabbling continuously amongst themselves for prime positions.

In the afternoon we return to the lions, finding them asleep sprawled across the shady side of the mound where we'd left them earlier. As the afternoon cools off the cubs and sub-adults become increasingly playful, the small cubs stalking and pouncing on their older siblings, who respond very gently and tolerantly. One small cub crosses to where its mother lies sleeping, then lies licking her head affectionately. The lions show little inclination to move before dark, and we watch later as the sun sinks slowly beneath the horizon, a brilliant red fireball.

1

September 24 We spend the morning on the floodplains and locate an aardwolf den in a deep hole. The aardwolf lies sunning itself in the entrance to the den, then retreats underground to sleep off its night's exertions as the sun climbs higher in the sky. Later we see a group of six elephant bulls swimming across the Zibadianja Lagoon, splashing and submerging completely at times. We decide this must be the origin of the expression 'having a whale of a time' for the huge behemoths certainly appear just like their marine counterparts, the massive ocean whales.

After a late lunch we head for the hippo pools again, finding a group of eight roan antelope at the water's edge when we arrive. The skittish antelope soon move off, but return later once we have parked the Land Rover, to drink at another section of the channel. Once again several breeding herds of elephant arrive at sunset and although it is too dark for photography, we enjoy watching them going about their activities.

2

5

3

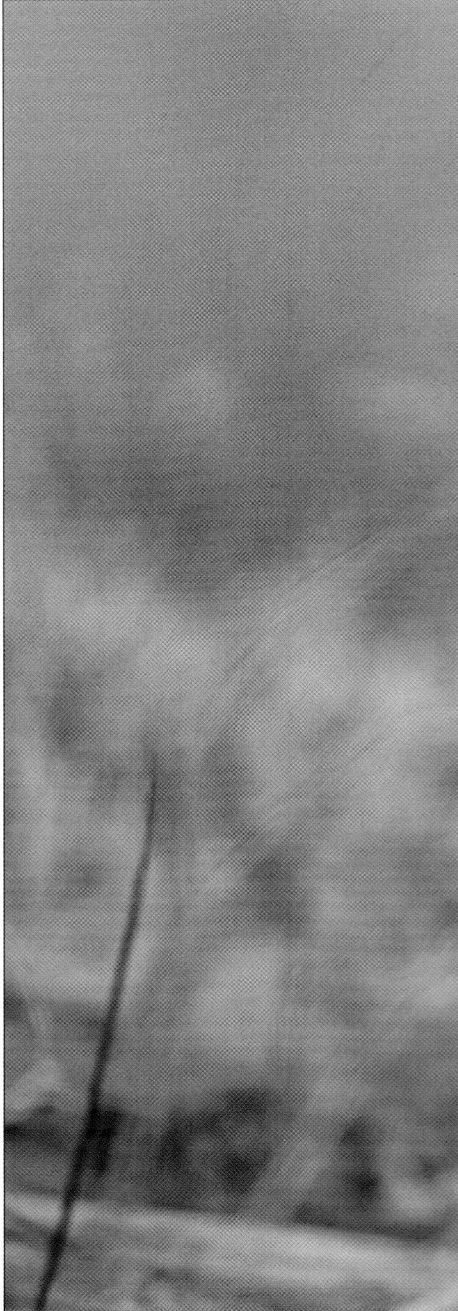

4

1 *Mutual grooming by cubs and their mothers enhances the social bonding in the family unit.*
2 *Ensnared by its mother's paws, the cub sleeps.*
3 *We find the Selinda Pride sprawled across the shady side of a large termite mound.*
4 *A lioness stares attentively from beneath the palm fronds.*
5 *Lying in the entrance to its den, the aardwolf barely flickers an eyelid as I crawl to within a metre of it.*
6 *A warthog kneels on its forelegs and digs for roots with its snout.*

6

September 25 In the late afternoon, we head out to the floodplains to the aardwolf den we have found, and find the aardwolf lying in the entrance. It seems quite relaxed when we drive up, having become accustomed to our vehicle during our recent visits. After photographing from the Land Rover, I crawl closer until I am lying less than a metre from the mouth of the den. Unperturbed, the aardwolf lies watching me, lying casually with its jaws resting on crossed forepaws. Even when I start using electronic flash in the fading evening light the animal barely reacts, cocking its head inquisitively from time to time. Only when darkness falls does the aardwolf stand up where it lies, shake itself off and trot away into the gloom. Thrilled by this wonderful encounter with one of Africa's rarely seen mammals, we return to camp for a celebratory dinner.

1 *Thirsty elephants jostle for water near midnight.*
2 *Much to this elephant's dismay the waterhole at Pump Pan is frequently dry.*
3 *The unrelenting sun beats down on the parched countryside.*
4 *The grasslands of the Savuti Marsh have been transformed into a dusty, windswept desertscape.*

SAVUTI — A HAZE OF HEAT AND DUST

September 27 We returned to our base camp in Savuti from Selinda yesterday, to find the area drier and more windswept than we have ever seen it before. Hardly a blade of grass survives and most of the trees are bare and apparently lifeless. The three artificial waterholes in the area remain busy around the clock and the main waterpoint, Pump Pan, is frequently dry. It is a heart-rending sight to visit the pan at midday and find upwards of a hundred elephants standing disconsolately around the dry waterhole, patiently waiting for the pumps to be switched on to bring them life-giving sustenance. The elephants stand in pathetic clusters in the scant shade offered by several large old camelthorn trees, their tails to the tree-trunk and heads facing out. Herds of impala and kudu approach the dry pan, then trudge away, thirsty still, on finding it empty. We call on the Department of Wildlife and National Parks offices to ascertain why the pump is not running, and are promised it will be attended to! Later on, with the water flowing steadily into the concrete pan, we spend the afternoon parked in close proximity to the elephants watching as they drink gratefully. A pack of wild dogs arrives, but cannot get close to the water. They lie sprawled in the dust nearby, awaiting a chance to drink once the elephants have slaked their giant thirsts.

We visit Lloyd's Camp for a birthday celebration dinner, then stop at Pump Pan on our way back to our own camp, near midnight. Still there are elephants jostling and shoving at the waterhole, though now we find two breeding herds with small calves, rare sightings around Savuti during the dry season, for these herds tend to move north to the Linyanti Swamp where water and grazing conditions are better.

1

September 29 With the onset of spring the sun rises early and it is before six when we set off from our camp en route to the Savuti Marsh. It couldn't look less like a marsh at present, appearing more like a desert with only a few tufts of brown, lifeless grass and drifts of windswept sand accentuated by the gaunt skeletons of the long-dead trees so characteristic of this area. Despite the dryness — no rain has fallen since April — the candlepod acacia shrubs are all in full bloom, their delightful pale yellow blossoms brightening the otherwise drab landscape and filling the air with a lovely fragrance. We see several herds of impala feeding on the blossoms and fresh green shoots that have begun sprouting on the thorny branches. Giraffe and elephant also feed on these prickly shrubs.

October 5 At Rhino Vlei we find six wild dogs and a puppy, still very bloody from a recent kill, lying scattered about the waterhole. There is a moment of excitement when several hyena come running in, one carrying the severed head of an impala, and rush straight into the water. The dogs immediately leap to their feet and make an effort to snatch the gory trophy from the hyena, but it wades deeper into the water until all that protrudes above the surface is its own head.This appears to be too deep for the wild dogs and they retreat to dry land. Two other hyenas enter the fray and a brief scuffle takes place, but the original hyena manages to defend his prize and begins eating at the water's edge. The dogs now appear disinterested, though the pup begs the adults repeatedly and one by one they regurgitate food for it. The hyena show interest in these proceedings and venture closer, but the six dogs keep a close watch and rush snarling at them whenever they get too close.

5

4

1 *With its trophy held securely, the hyena wades deeper into the water where the wild dogs won't follow.*
2 *Six wild dogs and a puppy lounge around the waterhole at Rhino Vlei.*
3 *Two of the dogs engage in a bout of fisticuffs.*
4 *An elephant carefully feeds thorny acacia shoots into its mouth.*
5 *An impala feeds on the blossoms and fresh green shoots that have sprouted from the candlepod acacia's prickly branches.*

2

3

1

2

3

4

October 7 The elephants have been without water at Pump Pan for the past two days, but still they stand about in disconsolate groups, apparently confident that if they wait long enough the water will come. We feel desperately sorry for the animals, and reflect that if conservation authorities decide to provide artificial waterpoints to keep game in certain areas they should be aware of their responsibilities to provide that water once the animals have become dependent on it. We count 66 elephants waiting for water, and see several of them actually sucking liquid from their stomachs, their trunks stuck deep into their mouths, which they then spray behind their ears to cool off. With midday temperatures well in excess of 42°C the elephants are feeling the heat for they are unable to cool off without water to drink or to spray over their bodies. The back of elephants' ears are covered with a vast network of blood vessels which aid in temperature regulation. By fanning their ears — and spraying them with water — they are able to keep their body temperature several degrees lower than would otherwise be possible.

Later that night, as we sit enjoying a cup of coffee under a nearly-full moon in our camp, several elephants appear out of the darkness, walking straight to where we sit. They have obviously been attracted by the scent of moisture and we watch as they explore the place where we have a small dish of water set out for the birds. Naturally the small basin does not contain enough to satisfy even a fraction of their thirst, but three trunks eagerly dip into it then toss it aside to scour the damp soil beneath.

1 *Savuti's elephants are dependent on the artificial water supply and when it dries up they wait in pathetic clusters under a shady tree, hoping the life-giving water will soon flow into the nearby pan.*

2 *As the drought continues, they stand about the dry pan, sucking with their trunks at the dried-up outflow pipes.*

3 *From time to time the elephants scuffle and shove at each other.*

4 *We watch amazed as an elephant draws water from its stomach, then sprays it behind its huge ears to cool its super-heated body.*

Left: *A bull elephant looms over us. Savuti is renowned for its tolerant and approachable elephant bulls, particularly at Pump Pan.*

October 8 We find Maome's Pride at Rhino Vlei on our early morning drive, and note that one lioness has a badly broken jaw, probably the legacy of a battle with buffalo. She does not seem much thinner than the other pride members, and even though she dribbles down her chest when drinking, appears to be managing with her injury. The pride are in poor condition, thin and with their coats dull and lifeless, but show scant interest when a herd of impala come to drink. The dominant lioness of the group, named 'Sloe-eyes' by the guides at Lloyd's Camp, comes to drink near where we have parked, and makes a perfect reflection in the still waters. She is still there when a young bull elephant arrives on the scene. He makes a brief, tentative charge and waves his trunk at the lioness but she is unfazed and merely snarls irritatedly and stands her ground. The elephant looks somewhat embarrassed at this, and chooses to drink further around the waterhole!

2

3

Returning to camp, we pack the Land Rover for a few nights at the Makapa Pans about an hour and a half to the east of Savuti, where we think the Sethlare Pride have moved, for they have not been seen in Savuti since the end of July. We travel along a sandy track through dense mopane woodland — along the southern route to the Nogatsaa and Tchinga area — and arrive at the first of the three main pans about midday. Apart from a few vultures sitting at the edge of the water and a loan roan antelope that canters away as we arrive, there is little activity and we continue to the second, larger pan a short distance further along. When we reach this pan we are rewarded with the sight of all the sub-adult males of the Sethlare Pride, sitting in the sparse shade of a leadwood tree. They are in magnificent condition and their bulging stomachs tell us they have only recently left a kill. We scout around the pan but see no sign of any lionesses or younger cubs, and wonder if these males have been evicted from the pride by the two big lions. Deciding to check the next pan, about five kilometres distant, we continue on our way and here we find Pandani and Othello, the two magnificently full-maned Sethlare lions, sleeping off the heat of the day in the shade of another leadwood. Sensing that nothing was likely to occur in the midday heat, we follow their cue and find a shady spot of our own, draping ourselves in wet cotton kikois (East African cloth wraps) to keep cool as the temperature rises to nearly 48°C.

5

4

1 *'Sloe-eyes', the dominant lioness of Maome's Pride, comes down to drink.*
2 *The candlepod acacias are now in full bloom, and fill the air with their scent.*
3 *The elephant makes a brief, tentative charge at the lioness, but she is unperturbed and merely snarls a reply.*
4 *An elephant cow and two youngsters arrive to quench their thirst at the muddy waterhole.*
5 *A lone roan antelope canters away as we arrive at Makapa Pans.*

October 9

We are awake long before sunrise and stow our bedding and other camping equipment before it is light. A few of the lions are at the waterhole, and we follow as they wander back towards where we know they have their kill. The lions soon disappear from sight in the thick scrub, but we scout around and find a few large bones obviously carried off by hyenas, then come across the fresh skull and horns of a magnificent eland bull. Eland *(Taurotragus oryx)* are the largest of all antelope and an adult male can weigh up to 800 kilograms, so it is no wonder the lions are looking so well fed.

Returning to the third pan, we find the two big lions have barely moved since yesterday, and discover a lone lioness nearby. She has an injured forefoot and limps away into the undergrowth when we approach, preventing us from getting close enough to identify her as one of the Sethlare Pride or not. The lions do not appear any less lazy than they were yesterday, and after watching us intently for a few minutes, flop on to their sides and go back to sleep.

We position ourselves to watch the waterhole and see a small herd of five roan antelope warily approaching. They can obviously smell the lions and are very nervous, circling around and walking to and fro for over an hour. Just as they are about to reach the water, a yellowbilled kite *(Milvus migrans)* swoops down from the sky near them and in panic they bolt back into the mopane. Roan antelope are so timid it is surprising they ever get to drink. Later, as the heat rises, several kudu, zebra, impala and eland, as well as the ubiquitous elephants come to drink, but the midday sunlight is too flat and harsh to warrant photography. In the evening we sit with the two lions, who again show little signs of activity, and later settle down for what turns out to be a very silent night.

1

2

3

4

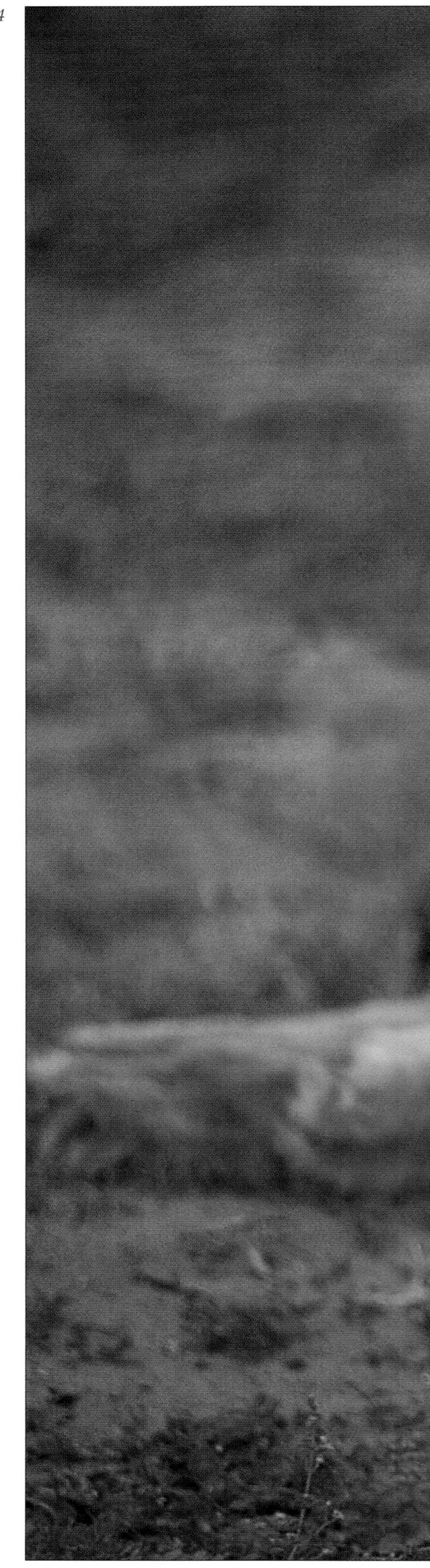

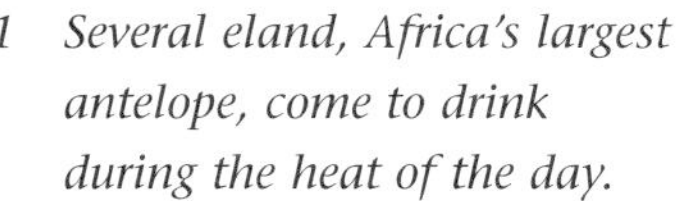

1 *Several eland, Africa's largest antelope, come to drink during the heat of the day.*
2 *Stretched out on his side, the lion shows little sign of activity in the torpid heat.*
3 *The lions do not appear any less lazy than yesterday.*
4 *Only when I alight from the vehicle to change the angle of photography does the lion raise his head and watch me with curiosity.*

1

ELEPHANTS OF CHOBE

October 13 Once again we take the long road north to the Chobe River at Serondella. October, the hottest and driest time of year in northern Botswana, sees huge concentrations of game, particularly elephant and buffalo, along the Chobe riverfront. Today is no exception and only minutes out of Kasane we encounter a huge herd bathing in the river. The elephants are being very noisy, trumpeting and squealing, and there are a large number of small calves which run around, splashing in the water and climbing atop each other. The smallest of the calves, perhaps only a week old, seems fascinated by the water. Too young to use its trunk, the calf kneels down to drink with its mouth, its tiny trunk curled back over its head. We spend more than an hour watching the elephants, then make our way into Kasane to collect mail and messages and do some shopping and vehicle maintenance. We return to the park as the sun is setting. There are herds of elephants everywhere along the waterfront, swimming, drinking and rolling in the mud and dust and a heavy dust haze hangs in the air above the elephants, turned golden by the last rays of sunlight.

2

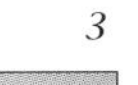

3

October 15 Leaving camp early, we find two lionesses with four youngsters out on the Chobe floodplain, then a big herd of buffalo moving away from the river into the surrounding scrub where they will spend the daylight hours. Backtracking along the riverfront, we drive west of Serondella and encounter another herd of buffalo several hundred strong, then see a small group of elephants drinking at a bend in the river. They, too, have a very young calf with them, still very unsteady on its feet and pink behind the ears. It loves the water, however, rolling and splashing with childlike glee. One of the adults, a tuskless cow, sees us and approaches aggressively, 'standing tall' in the typical threat posture, her ears spread wide. She then turns abruptly and with a low rumble leads the herd away, the smallest calves tucked protectively between the adults' legs. Deciding to treat ourselves to Sunday brunch, we head for the luxurious Chobe Game Lodge and feast on a splendid breakfast buffet, then relax in the hotel's cool lounge for the remainder of the morning while catching up on correspondence.

5

4

1 *Chobe is famous for its elephants. Here a number of small calves run around playing and climbing atop each other.*
2 *The tip of the African elephant's trunk comprises two dextrous 'fingers'.*
3 *The main herd crosses the river towards Namibia, while a few small calves bob alongside as though towed in the wake.*
4 & 5 *A heavy haze of dust, coloured by the setting sun, hangs in the air above the elephants that throng the shores of the Chobe River before nightfall.*
6 *We spare a thought for the subsistence farmers on the Namibian side of the river, whose crops will doubtless take a beating tonight.*

6

Later we head for the riverside again and see a large herd of elephants about to cross the Chobe River to the Namibian side. The elephants mass on the river bank, then plunge into the water. Unfortunately there are eight different powerboats from the various safari camps and lodges in close attendance, some venturing too close for the elephants' comfort. A small calf panics and turns back, flailing awkwardly in the water, and re-emerges on to the bank. Its mother turns back and also leaves the water, appearing to have some difficulty in convincing her youngster to re-enter the water. Eventually the boats back off and depart, allowing mother and child to make a safe though belated crossing, joining their herd on the far side.

1

October 17 Leaving camp just after sunrise we head for the Chobe Game Lodge where we have made arrangements to use a small boat to photograph waterbirds. We head downstream to a sandbar where we photograph a pair of African skimmers *(Rynchops flavirostris)*, a flock of African spoonbills *(Platalea alba)* and a lesser jacana *(Microparra capensis)*. Later we find the lions again, sleeping in some bushes near the river.

5

October 18 After we left them last night the lions killed a baby elephant, a speciality of the Chobe lions, and we are quite happy we did not stay with them. We have spent four years studying and photographing elephants and feel too much of an affinity for them to want to photograph, or even see, a small calf being pulled down by lions. We make a quick trip to Kasane to buy fuel, then on our return find a herd of 53 sable antelope at the water's edge on Watercart Loop, a popular game drive track along the waterfront.

In the afternoon we again find a large herd of elephants gathering on the river bank preparing to cross to the Namibian side after nightfall. This time there are no boats about and the elephants cross at their leisure, enjoying the swim, submerging entirely at times and then surfacing with huge spouts of water expelled from their trunks. It appears that the smallest calves, which stay very close to their mothers, are actually towed along by the wake created by the adults. Later we see another herd making its way towards the river, and spare a moment's sympathy for the Namibian subsistence farmers on the far side whose crops will take a beating tonight. Meanwhile the culprits will be safely back in Chobe by daybreak! We reflect on the fact that the biggest threat to elephant populations comes not so much from hunting and poaching, but rather from conflict with ever-increasing human populations for space in which to carry on their lives. Unless steps are taken to curb mankind's own apparently unfettered population growth there seems little chance that any wild species or places will ultimately survive.

4

2

3

1 Returning along Watercart Loop, we encounter a large herd of sable antelope.

2 We head downstream by boat, and photograph a co-operative lesser jacana, some African skimmers (5) and a flock of African spoonbills (3).

4 Two young bull elephants engage in a watery wrestling match in a quiet backwater off the main Chobe River.

As the sun sets amid a palette of red and pink hues, we see a large leopard tortoise (Geochelone pardalis) *making its way across the grassy floodplain. According to local legend this is a sign of impending rain.*

1

October 21 It is cloudy and windy when we rise, and we spend the morning frustrated by the poor photographic conditions. The afternoon turns out somewhat better, however, and we spend a fruitful two hours photographing a co-operative Chobe bushbuck ram *(Tragelaphus scriptus ornatus)* just outside the national park gates. Across the river channel, on the disputed Sedudu Island (both Namibia and Botswana have laid claim to this piece of land mid-stream in the Chobe River, Botswana currently maintaining a prominent military presence on the island) we see a big buffalo herd grazing contentedly on the lush grasses, along with a few elephants. Returning to our camp along the waterfront we enjoy a spectacular sunset with several elephants in the foreground, then encounter the big elephant herd crossing the river to Namibia at the same place once again.

October 24 We find a pride of nine lions feeding on a buffalo kill near the river, looking replete and satisfied. Realising they are unlikely to move during the day we continue with our drive, seeing several puku and waterbuck, as well as a small herd of roan antelope. After lunch we return to the lions, which eventually rise and move off a short distance, then settle down again. We leave them to drive down on to the floodplain, where we can see several herds of elephants dust-bathing and feeding on the nutritious short grasses growing there. The setting sun filters through the thick dust clouds kicked up by the elephants, making for a spectacular sunset (p. 99).

2

3

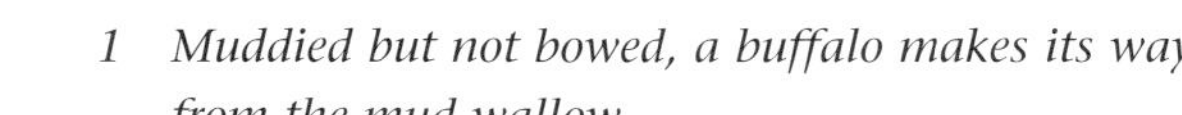

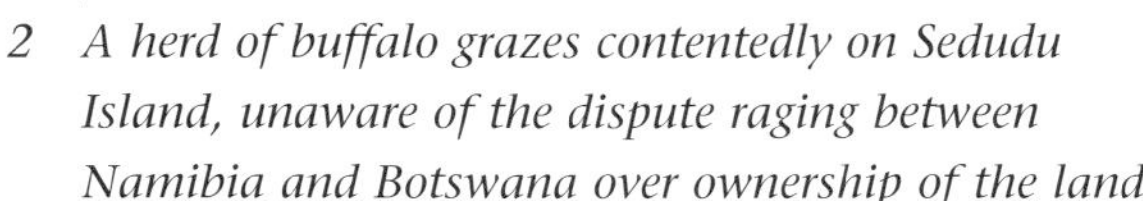

1 *Muddied but not bowed, a buffalo makes its way from the mud wallow.*

2 *A herd of buffalo grazes contentedly on Sedudu Island, unaware of the dispute raging between Namibia and Botswana over ownership of the land.*

3 *A co-operative Chobe bushbuck ram poses nervously in front of the camera.*

4 *Vultures bicker and fight over the spoils of death.*

5 *The pride feeds on a buffalo they have pulled down alongside the river. Chobe's lions are renowned for hunting buffalo and elephant calves.*

4

5

1

2

3

4

1 A lone elephant bull feeds alongside the river as the sun sets.
2 A young cow stands protectively alongside a small elephant calf.
3 The Chobe River is home to some of Botswana's largest crocodiles.
4 Waterbuck are commonly seen along the Chobe waterfront.
5 A warthog boar looms large in this wide-angle image!

October 28 There are elephants wherever we look around Chobe. Along the riverfront, in the riverine forest, up on the sandridge overlooking the Chobe floodplain and further inland in the teak forests. All have moved towards the river, for now this is the only water available to them. Every day brings promise of rain — clouds build up on the horizon, the wind gusts in threatening squalls and at night sheet lightning flickers in the distance. Everyone we meet has an opinion on when the rains will come and whether they will be good or bad, early or late.

Later in the evening, as we sit around the campfire making dinner, lightning flashes across the river and the wind brings the fresh smell of rain on dry earth to us. We have been sleeping under the stars on the roof of the Land Rover most nights, but now we decide prudence dictates we should erect a tent, for as we talk the wind rises and the rain comes closer. When we retire for the evening we take a bucket of fresh water to wash the Serondella dust from our feet before slipping into bed, then leave the bucket of dirty water standing outside the doorway of the tent, which we decide to leave open to facilitate the movement of air, and fall asleep.

Some hours later we awaken to the sound of lapping at the doorway. Slowly I reach for a torch, flicking it on as we both sit up on the mattress. There, inches from the open doorway — and our feet — stand five lion cubs and behind them two lionesses. The wide-eyed cubs stand transfixed in the torchlight, then carry on drinking the soapy water unconcernedly. Eventually the lionesses walk away and the cubs follow, barely glancing back in our direction as they wander out of the camp area. We watch them disappear into the night and go back to sleep, exhilarated by the encounter. In the morning we find a full can of beer alongside the bucket, dented slightly by the lions' teeth. It is obvious that the cats had visited the campsite alongside ours first and had picked up the beer there, then set it down when they drank our water. A fair deal, we considered!

5

SUMMER

The coming of the rains

When storm clouds begin to build and gather, and lightning arcs across supercharged skies, there's a tangible aura of excitement in the air.

Drought is no stranger to Botswana, and the summer rains fail more often than not. Semi-arid, semi-desert, drought-stricken ... they are all terms which apply equally to this vast land. Thus the imminent coming of the rains — or the possibility of their non-arrival — is the main topic of conversation as spring passes into summer and the skies stubbornly remain cloudless. Then, slowly the clouds begin to mass, darkening the distant horizon. Day by day the clouds gather, heavier and darker now, and we can smell the rains when the wind blows towards us. The first teasing showers do little more than settle the dust however, and then only for a few hours until the unrelenting sun beats down once more. Isolated thunderstorms, lightning arcing dramatically across the superheated skies, bring slight relief, filling temporary pools and puddles with sweet rainwater much appreciated by the long-suffering wildlife. Many of the animals are now heavily pregnant, the impala in particular wait for the onset of the rains to drop their young. Although we see a few lambs among the impala herds it is obvious these are early arrivals, their mothers perhaps fooled into thinking the first few showers were the precursors of the main rains.

Above: *Storm clouds gather as spring becomes summer.*
Left: *With the coming of the rains the lions begin to show renewed vigour, for they know the season of plenty will soon be here.*

1

November 25 A good shower during the night means we waken to a glittering morning, raindrops hanging like jewels from the grass and leaves wherever we look. We head down the track to the Savuti Marsh, now at least beginning to look less like the desert it was during the dry winter, splashing through deep puddles as we drive. The sky above is clear, however, a few wispy cirrus clouds all that break the monotony of the vast eggshell-blue expanse. We see more and more summer migrants: European bee-eaters *(Merops apiaster)*, lesser striped swallows *(Hirunda abyssinica)* and woodland kingfishers *(Halcyon senegalensis)* among the most readily noticeable. At last the countryside is taking on its summer colours — where only a few weeks ago all was drab and brown, now fresh green grasses carpet the landscape and the trees are in full leaf. We find several small groups of zebra feeding on the marsh, and this morning the few tsessebe are in high spirits, racing back and forth and chasing one another round in circles, no doubt cheered by the night's rain.

5

November 29 Several good rain showers over the past two nights have brought respite to the area again, though regulars like Lloyd Wilmot still maintain the 'real rains' have not yet arrived. There is now water lying everywhere and pans that have not held a drop since May are filling rapidly. Importantly, the skies remain dull and overcast, preventing the sun from evaporating too much of the precipitation. More zebra are arriving in the area, beginning their migration from their winter range along the Linyanti, and several pockets of wildebeest are also out on the marsh. The elephants have perked up considerably, striding across the landscape with a spring in their step now where prior to the rains they trudged wearily.

2

1 The onset of the rains is a time of renewal and many species give birth to their young.
2 Seasonal pans that have not held water since May are quickly filled.
3 A flock of cattle egrets whirl and wheel over a pocket of wildebeest on the marsh.
4 Even the tree squirrels seem excited at the coming of the wet season.
5 We see more and more summer migrants, like this European bee-eater.

3

4

1

December 1 Another cloudy, dull dawn greets us and we spend a quiet morning around the marsh. There are a few zebra foals with the herds now, but no more newborn impala lambs. We spend the rest of the afternoon at Pump Pan with the elephants, which take their time drinking and bathing at leisure.

December 2 Once again the day is grey and dismal, the cloud base very low and threatening. The zebra are massing in greater numbers now, and there seem to be more elephants about than a month ago. By mid-afternoon a big storm is brewing and we rush around camp making certain everything is secure. Then the storm hits, deafening thunder crashes and great streaks of lightning slashing the dark sky while the rain comes down in buckets. The storm is awesome, sheets of rain cutting visibility to a few metres and a raging wind whipping the treetops to a frenzy. It rains on unabated into the night, only slowing sometime in the early hours. Later, in a moment of quiet, we hear the roars of the Sethlare Pride ... they have returned to Savuti at last.

December 3 It still rains gently when we rise, and the world around us is sodden. Rivulets of water gush down the track into the bed of the Savuti Channel, and we fantasize about the possibility of the long-dry watercourse flowing once again during our stay. The channel has been dry since the early 1980s, but it will take more than a few downpours to get it flowing again. By late morning the rain has abated and we see a few blue patches in the sky, so we leave camp to explore the surroundings. Driving away from camp we encounter the resident impala herd and immediately notice that where yesterday there were none, today there are at least a dozen newborn lambs lying in the wet grass or standing about on unsteady legs!

2

1 & 2 The elephants take their time drinking, bathing and interacting at leisure.
3 A line of zebras files across the marsh as rain clouds build up in the distance.
4 & 5 Where yesterday there were none, today we notice at least a dozen newborn impala lambs, suckling from their mothers and standing about on spindly legs.

3

4

5

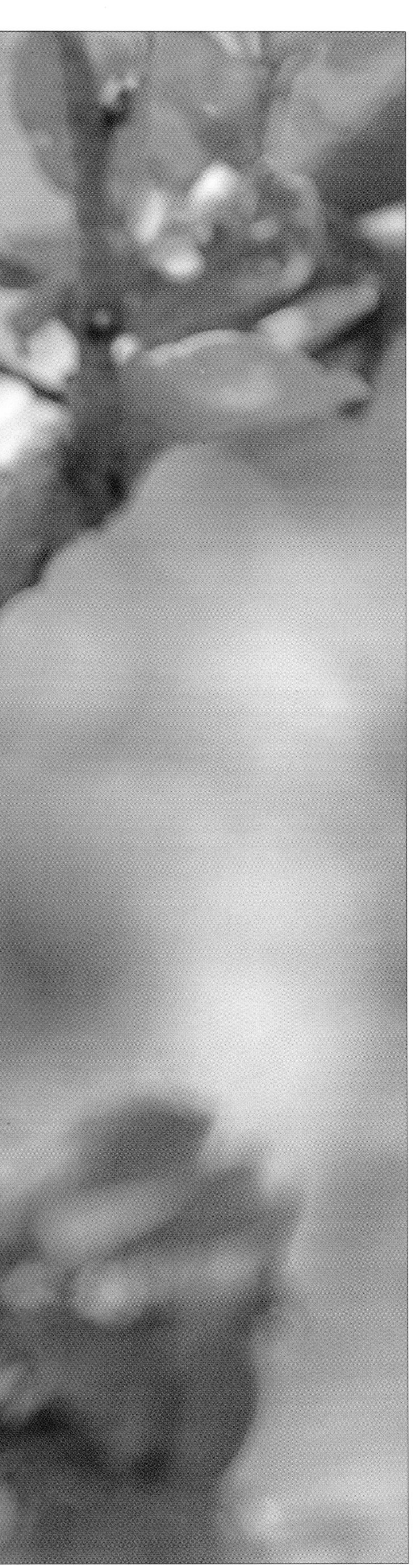

1

2

3

1 *A nest almost overflowing with four white-crowned shrike chicks.*
2 *We see a herd of tsessebe with their first calf of the season.*
3 *There are more buffalo in the area now, feeding along the eastern side of the marsh.*
4 *The zebra are beginning to gather, while once again the clouds build up in the east.*

December 6 It rains off and on continuously now and the game is becoming very scattered. There is little activity out on the marsh and it appears most of the game may have moved into the surrounding woodlands for shelter from the incessant rains. The marsh gets greener by the day, and there are several areas where it is becoming very wet and swampy, much as it would have been in the days when the Savuti Channel still flowed and it was a true marsh. There are more buffalo in the area now, particularly on the eastern side of the marsh fringing the mopane woodland.

December 7 Once again we hear the Sethlare Pride roaring loudly near the camp before dawn, but rise and head straight for the marsh, hoping to photograph it in its flooded state after heavy overnight rain. The sun is shining brightly for a change, with barely a cloud in the sky, but when we reach the marsh we find the rain has already soaked away. We see a herd of several tsessebe with their first calf of the season and spend the next four hours patiently — and unsuccessfully — watching another tsessebe which appears to be close to calving too. Later in the afternoon we photograph a nest almost overflowing with four whitecrowned shrike nestlings *(Eurocephalus anguittimens)*, then find several herds of zebra grazing on the marsh near Motsibi Island as rain clouds gather in the distance once more.

4

December 8 At last we have found the Sethlare Pride again, all looking very fat and glossy-coated, resting off the track near Peter's Pan. One of the young males finds a tortoise in the grass and soon there is a game in progress among several of the sub-adults, each trying to take possession of the strange creature and struggling — unsuccessfully — to gain access to the animal within! As the sun begins to set the lions rise and move towards the pan, but when they cross a very wet, marshy area we are unable to follow for fear of becoming stuck and lose them in the gathering gloom.

December 10 We find the marsh covered with zebra as far as the eye can see ... at last the migration has started. Driving through the bunched herds we still see very few foals, for the main foaling season is later in the summer, but we do encounter a herd of wildebeest with a very new calf, still wet and with its umbilical cord hanging down.

December 12 Last night while out on the marsh tracking lions we came across a jackal den, and we head there at first light. There are three cute little jackal puppies, and after a while they emerge to lie in the sun watching us. Both mom and dad jackal stay close by, preening each other from time to time, apparently unconcerned by our presence. The wildebeest herds on the marsh have a few more young with them now, but we are unable to find any of them in labour.

1

2

3

4

1 *Now and then the two jackals groom each other.*
2 *One of the pups wanders off from the den to join its mother alongside an old tree-stump.*
3 *The jackal puppies lie watching us when we stop nearby.*
4 *One of the young lions attempting, unsuccessfully, to gain access to the creature inside the shell.*

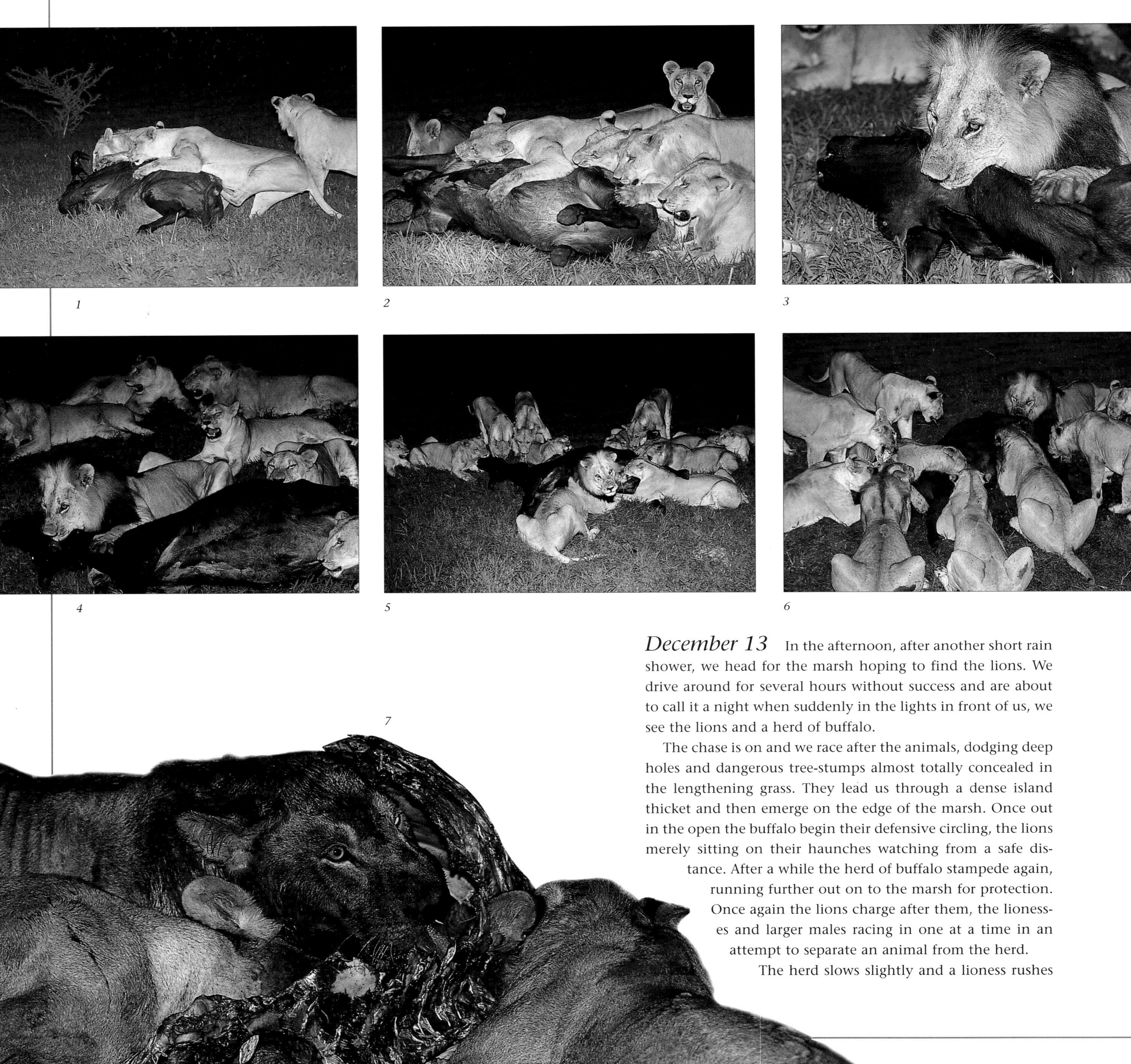

1

2

3

4

5

6

7

December 13 In the afternoon, after another short rain shower, we head for the marsh hoping to find the lions. We drive around for several hours without success and are about to call it a night when suddenly in the lights in front of us, we see the lions and a herd of buffalo.

The chase is on and we race after the animals, dodging deep holes and dangerous tree-stumps almost totally concealed in the lengthening grass. They lead us through a dense island thicket and then emerge on the edge of the marsh. Once out in the open the buffalo begin their defensive circling, the lions merely sitting on their haunches watching from a safe distance. After a while the herd of buffalo stampede again, running further out on to the marsh for protection. Once again the lions charge after them, the lionesses and larger males racing in one at a time in an attempt to separate an animal from the herd.

The herd slows slightly and a lioness rushes

in, pouncing on to the back of a large buffalo cow, which bellows loudly in distress. The herd immediately swings around and charges menacingly at the lions, which break ranks and flee before them. Realising that attack is the better form of defence, the buffalo now chase after the fleeing lions, which scatter in all directions. Having repelled their attackers the buffalo veer off and continue to run out on to the marsh. Though the lions turn and give chase, they have all but lost the initiative and soon give up, panting heavily with all the exertion. The buffalo are too wary to pursue further.

Suddenly a lone buffalo cow emerges from the treeline and makes a bee-line for the rest of the herd. The cow was obviously left behind in the initial chase and is now attempting to rejoin them. Then, close on her heels, we see one of the two Sethlare Pride male lions emerge from the trees. He lopes along behind her, and the buffalo seems unaware of his presence. Meanwhile the rest of the lion pride also appear oblivious of the lone buffalo and proceed to walk towards a small knoll, where they seem intent on resting and regaining their breath. Suddenly though, one of the younger cubs spies the approaching buffalo and alerts the others. The lionesses immediately rush forward in the darkness, dropping to the ground when they see the buffalo heading straight for them. With bated breath we watch the drama unfold in front of us, illuminating the scene with a dim red light so as not to interfere with the eyesight of either the lions or the buffalo. The buffalo trots towards us, and several lionesses lie in ambush in the grass less than 20 metres away.

The buffalo walks straight into the trap. The biggest of the lionesses leaps to her feet and pounces on the cow's back. When another lioness jumps on to its shoulders the buffalo crashes to the ground **(1 & 2)**, kicking furiously. The big lion, which we identify as Othello, races in and immediately clenches the struggling buffalo's windpipe in his crushing jaws **(3)**, slowly strangling the powerful animal. Exhausted after all the exertion, the rest of the pride run up, but flop in a semi-circle around the kill **(4)** to recover their energy and breath before commencing feeding. It takes at least 10 minutes for the buffalo to die, and when the lion moves to start eating his share **(5)** the others give way respectfully. Later Pandani, the second big male, arrives, but only starts feeding on the carcass when Othello has eaten his fill.

Although it takes little over two hours for the pride to consume the major portion of the buffalo **(6)**, they stay with the kill all night, feeding intermittently **(7 & 8)** until just after sunrise when only a few bare bones and the horns are all that remain for the few jackal that wait patiently nearby **(9)**.

9

8

1

December 14 We leave the lions resting in a grove of trees and return to camp to catch up on our own sleep, only returning to the marsh in the late afternoon. We find the lions grooming one another where we had left them, their bellies heavy and bloated. Although we consider the chances of another kill to be slim so soon after the pride have consumed a whole buffalo, we follow when they move on to the marsh shortly after sundown. A short while later a lioness flushes a springhare and gives chase, a long and high-speed jinking effort that she eventually wins, trotting off proudly with the small animal struggling haplessly in her jaws. This seems to incite the other lions, and they chase after a lone impala ewe which successfully evades their claws, only to round a bush and run straight into Othello. He grabs it triumphantly, and snarls aggressively when any other pride members approach. Then the lionesses flush an impala lamb from the long grass, probably the offspring of the impala Othello is now feeding on. The chase is over quickly and the lamb is ripped to shreds and devoured within minutes. Next the lions disturb a spotted dikkop *(Burhinus capensis)* where it roosts in the grass and leaping acrobatically into the air, one of the sub-adult males catches the bird as it attempts to fly to safety.

We are astounded by the lions' prodigious appetites, for they can hardly have finished digesting last night's buffalo, yet they seem intent on gorging themselves on anything they can catch tonight. We continue following them, but when they head into thick mopane and Kalahari appleleaf *(Lonchocarpus nelsii)* we lose track of them. Just then the rain begins to pelt down and after backtracking a way we find Pandani alone on the marsh, scent-marking every bush he passes and roaring defiantly to all who will listen. The rain continues unabated, and after seeing a lone cheetah cowering in the grass, no doubt petrified by the nearby lion's roars, we decide to retire to the dryness of our tents.

5

2

1 *Several of the lions climb into the branches of a fallen tree, scanning the darkness ahead of them.*

2 *A springhare, flushed by a lioness, takes off across the open plains with the predator in hot pursuit.*

3 *The lions lounge about, bellies bloated, as the sun sets in the distance.*

4 & 5 *The impala runs around a bush straight into the waiting lion, which grabs it and drags it off to one side to eat.*

3

4

December 15 We find the lions sleeping near where we left them last night, then continue on our way before finding several elephants feeding among the yellow flowering devil's thorn creepers *(Tribulus zeyheri)*. Later in the day we return to the lions, which move off soon after sundown and make several unsuccessful attempts at hunting zebra. When the pride reaches the western marsh road they turn south, following the track for several kilometres before heading back out on the marsh.

One lioness, who we have named the 'Huntress' for her skills, leaves the pride and moves on ahead while the others lie resting. About 10 minutes later the pride rises suddenly and moves off quickly, with us following by the light of the moon. The lions have become so used to our presence over the months that it seems almost as though they regard the Land Rover as one of the pride. They frequently rest in its shade during the day, use it as a rallying point, rub their heads against the brush-guard and often wait for us to catch up when traversing across country. When following them at night we can often drive so close that our fender almost touches their flanks, enabling us to remain literally in touch in the dark. After a while the pride regroups, then the senior lionesses move off, the sub-adults remaining sprawled in the short grass around the Land Rover. We scan the countryside quickly with the red spotlight and pick out a herd of wildebeest in the distance, then sit quietly waiting in the blackness. Suddenly the quiet is broken by the sound of racing hooves, and the lions spring into action. We switch on the red light and spot the Huntress and the other lionesses in hot pursuit of about 30 wildebeest, with the sub-adults now bringing up the rear. We start up and follow as

1

1 A lone elephant feeds among the yellow flowers of the devil's thorn creeper (6).
2 The Huntress and another of the lionesses wrestle a wildebeest to the ground.
3 She clamps her jaws tightly over the muzzle, suffocating it quickly.
4 The rest of the pride begin feeding even before she has finished administering the coup de grâce.
5 The lions tuck into the feast, feeding voraciously.

2

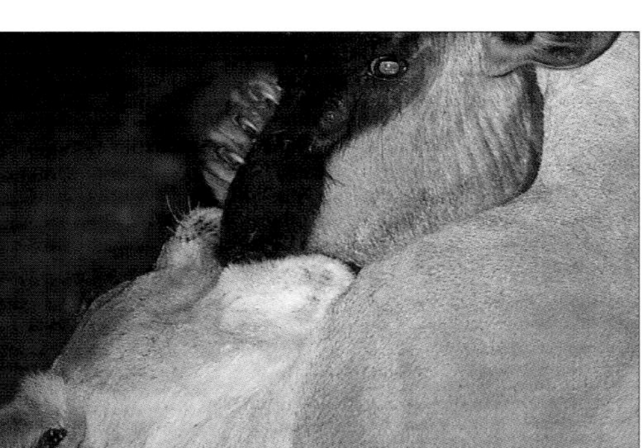
3

4

5

6

quickly as we can, watching as first one then another wildebeest is pulled down, snarling lions clinging to their flanks. We draw up alongside one of them, photographing as the lionesses wrestle their victim to the ground, then administer the coup de grâce. Less than 30 metres away we see several of the other lions with the second wildebeest we'd seen going down, while further away we pick out yet another carcass covered with the tawny predators.

We notice that all three of the wildebeest downed by the lions were heavily pregnant, and stay with the pride for several hours as they feed, both enthralled and appalled at their apparent viciousness and greed.

1

December 17 It rained heavily again most of yesterday and throughout the night, and we awaken to a dull grey day. We spend the morning resting in camp, catching up on chores and reinforcing the rainwater trenches around our tents. In the late afternoon the sun shows signs of emerging from behind the clouds and we head out to the marsh in search of the lions. We find them all at Motsibi Island, behaving very playfully and three of the youngsters clambering in and out of the branches of a small tree. Later the sun breaks through and lights up a stunning sunset sky with brilliant oranges, reds and pastel shades, against which we photograph several of the pride (back cover and title page). The lions move off soon after dark and we follow. In quick succession they kill a zebra foal, impala lamb and another zebra foal, then lie down to sleep in a closely huddled group. A cold wind has sprung up after the latest rains and we envy the lions their apparent cosiness. When after several hours they show no signs of further activity for the night we depart for our own beds.

5

December 19 After resting throughout the daylight hours, a spectacular sunset with the lions starts our evening, then we fall into our routine of follow and observe. The lions cross the marsh, stopping at one stage while one of the sub-adult males digs furiously in a futile attempt to excavate a springhare from its hole. The pride makes four unsuccessful attempts at killing zebra and we come to the conclusion that perhaps the lionesses are teaching their offspring how to hunt this species, for they persist in the pursuit of zebra even though there are several large herds of buffalo in the area, in which they show no interest.

2

1 *Several of the young lions clamber in the branches of a small tree.*
2 *A lone elephant bull drifts past as the sinking sun casts shafts of colour against distant clouds.*
3 *Two sub-adult lions take time off to lick each other clean. Such mutual grooming forms part of the bonding process.*
4 *The pride huddles cosily together against the cold wind that has sprung up.*
5 *In quick succession the lions kill an impala lamb and two zebra foals.*

3

4

A young lioness of the Sethlare Pride strikes an elegant pose against the spectacular backdrop of a dark blue, stormy sky, prior to joining her pridemates in the nocturnal hunt. Lions remain fully dependent on their natal pride until about 18 months of age, at least, but must fight for their share at a kill. Hungry mothers will deprive even their own offspring of food if need be.

1

6

December 23 Savuti is looking spectacular at the moment, lush and green with wildflowers everywhere. Every waterhole is full and ducks, geese and other waterbirds take advantage of this seasonal time of abundance. There are countless zebra on the marsh, though the herds are now more scattered than a few days ago, and elephants wherever we look. All the antelope have young now, and we see increasing numbers of zebra and wildebeest foals and calves with the herds. Driving out to the marsh in the late evening, we pass at least 50 elephants along the route, then find the Sethlare Pride lying just off the marsh road near Marabou Pan. It is still light when we see several groups of zebra heading towards where the lions lie, and the big cats immediately flatten themselves in the grass and move into ambush positions. We watch intently, certain we are about to see our first successful zebra hunt, when suddenly one of the younger cubs becomes impatient with all the silence and inactivity, stands up in full view of the approaching zebra and pounces playfully on one of his older siblings. The zebra stop and stare in utter amazement, then turn and gallop away. Much later the lions manage to down several zebra foals, but we sense that these are poor substitutes for the meal they had so narrowly missed.

December 24 Christmas Eve is celebrated in fine style with family and friends who have joined us in Savuti. After an early morning drive, during which we see a pair of klipspringer *(Oreotragus oreotragus)* perched on the side of Bushman Paintings Hill, several elephants and the Sethlare Pride, as well as a spectacular crowned crane *(Balearica regulorum)*, we return to camp for a relaxing afternoon, and to prepare the feast for dinner — roast turkey, roast lamb, a gammon ham and all the trimmings, all prepared on the open fire in traditional cast iron pots.

2

3

4

5

1 *Savuti is looking splendid after the summer rains, with wildflowers sprouting everywhere.*
2 *We spot a pair of klipspringer perched on the side of the koppie.*
3 *There are mounting numbers of wildebeest calves among the herds.*
4 *The Sethlare Pride males are in fine fettle, thanks to the benign conditions of the early rainy season.*
5 *A spectacular crowned crane strides across the marsh.*
6 *There are elephants wherever you look around Savuti, taking advantage of the nutritious new grasses that have sprouted across the marsh.*

December 29 Refreshed after a good night's sleep, we leave camp soon after sunrise and find a Bradfield's hornbill *(Tockus bradfieldi)* feeding its mate, cemented into a nest in a dead tree. Hornbills usually build their nests in natural holes in trees which the female then seals from within with mud and other material supplied by the male, leaving a narrow vertical slit through which her mate feeds her. As the young grow, the female breaks out of the nest, which is once again plastered closed by the young, who are then fed by both parents.

We watch the male flying back and forth for almost an hour, bringing an assortment of food such as large black dung-beetles, moths and butterflies, grasshoppers and even a small snake, which are all taken through the feeding slit by his mate within the nest.

We continue on our way and find a family of ground hornbills *(Bucorvus leadbeateri)* out on Wild Dog Vlei. There are several adults as well as a juvenile in the process of transformation from sub-adult to adult coloration, its facial and gular skin a pretty mottled yellow with reddish flecks rather than the bright red of the adults. The birds are foraging across the vlei, feeding on a variety of insects, beetles and frogs. Ground hornbills are entirely carnivorous and will eat almost anything including small tortoises, reptiles and even small mammals up to the size of hares.

Leaving the hornbills we find a small puddle in the process of drying out, leaving several hundred small tadpoles stranded high and dry. After photographing them we take pity and carefully transfer them to a larger pool nearby.

We spend the afternoon around Harvey's Pans, which are very full after all the rains, attracting numerous waterbirds and waders. The plains are looking very lush and there are wild mushrooms and flowers blooming everywhere. Later, as we sit observing a large flock of redwinged pratincoles *(Glareola pratincola)* roosting around one of the pans, we see several impala running panic-stricken out of the nearby mopane scrub, and drive over to investigate. We find a pack of wild dogs which have killed two impala lambs, though not much remains to be seen after the typical wild dog feeding frenzy.

1 *The wild dogs have killed two impala lambs.*
2 *Wild mushrooms and flowers have sprung up everywhere.*
3 *The plains are awash with colour — flowers, birds and countless butterflies.*
4 *Several tadpoles left stranded in a dried out puddle.*
5 *A Bradfield's hornbill brings food to his mate, sealed into her nest in a hollow dead tree.*
6 *Adult ground hornbills have bright red gular sacs.*

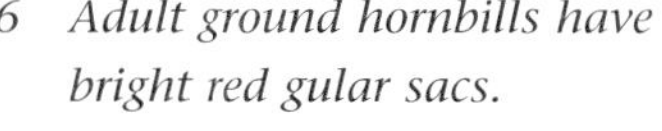

1

December 31 The last day of the year breaks clear and sunny, and we head out early to the Linyanti Plains at the back of Pump Pan. We are astonished to see fresh hippo tracks leading down the sandy road for there have been no resident hippo in Savuti since the Savuti Channel dried up more than a decade ago. After all the rain of the past month, it must have been encouraged to follow the dry course of the channel downstream from the hippo pools at Selinda over 100 kilometres away. There is certainly enough grazing for it at present, while all the pans are full, offering plenty of daytime places of refuge.

We then spot three different families of bat-eared fox on the plains, two of which appear very nervous at our approach, the third hardly looking up when we drive nearer. While watching the foxes we see an African wild cat slinking into a small clump of mopane, and move closer. The cat remains crouched in the bush, its camouflage making it nearly invisible if it were not for the glint of sunlight catching one of its eyes. Although we wait quietly for some time, the cat shows no intention of emerging from its hideout and we leave it in peace, preferring not to stress the timid animal with our continued presence.

January 1 We sleep in after a festive night celebrating the New Year at the nearby Gametrackers' Allan's Camp, then drive out to Harvey's Pans where we find the hippo ensconced in a deep pool. He surfaces to have a sleepy look at us, then submerges totally, only his nostrils remaining above the water and remains out of sight. We decide to name him 'Happy' in honour of New Year's day, then continue with our drive.

On the eastern marsh road we find Othello and one of the Sethlare Pride lionesses, both looking very satisfied with their courtship, but little other game is about, and we return to camp. In the afternoon we return to Harvey's Pan, where 'Happy the Hippo' performs well for us, yawning, splashing and blowing spouts of spray through his nostrils in perfect afternoon light.

5

2

3

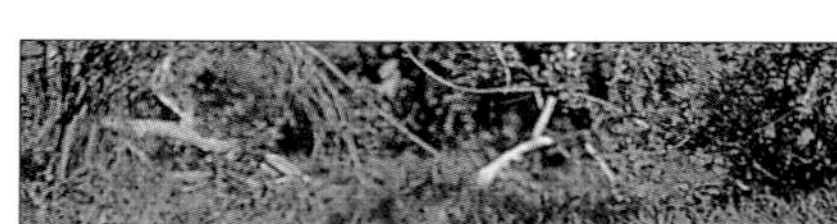

4

1 The African wild cat's camouflage makes it nearly invisible.

2 The bat-eared foxes nervously watch our approach.

3 Wild dogs enjoy bathing, and frequently wade chest deep into the water to drink and cool off.

4 The hippo surfaces to have a sleepy look at us.

5 & 6 In the afternoon we return to the hippo which performs well for us, splashing and yawning in the early evening light.

6

1

January 4 There has been no more rain since the brief shower on Christmas Eve and the days remain sunny and hot. Already the lush green grass on the marsh is yellowing and wilting in the heat and most of the zebra have departed for the Mababe Depression further to the southeast. But while much of the game has left Savuti, the area has been transformed into a bird paradise, many in breeding plumage and others with nests and small chicks. There are huge flocks of European swallows *(Hirundo rustica)* about now, as well as numbers of bluecheeked *(Merops persicus)* as well as European *(Merops apiaster)* and carmine *(Merops nubicoides)* bee-eaters. We also observe large numbers of both eastern *(Falco amurensis)* and western *(Falco vespertinus)* redfooted kestrels swooping around the plains and catching insects in the grass, but they prove to be very timid and elusive when we attempt to photograph them.

We find the Sethlare Pride near Marabou Pan in the late afternoon. Othello's courtship with the lioness appears to be over, for both he and Pandani lie some distance away from the rest of the pride, who are scattered about in the shade of a candlepod acacia bush, while one of the lionesses lies casually draped in the branches of a dead tree that has fallen over nearby. Later several other lions join her in the tree, clambering about and using it as a vantage point to overlook the nearby open plains, which are depressingly bare at present.

4

January 6 At last it rains heavily again, a good downpour in mid-afternoon that once again seems to rejuvenate the area. 'Happy the Hippo' has recently been joined by two others, and they seem to occupy various waterholes on the Linyanti Plains and Harvey's Pans on a rotational basis. We have also located several dwarf bitterns *(Ixobrychus sturmii)*, a rare sighting in this area, including a nesting pair who have built their flimsy nest, a platform of sticks, twigs and grass, in a tree overhanging Poacher's Pan. We visit the nest hoping to find one of the nesting pair sitting in the open sun after the rain, to no avail, and we drive on to the Linyanti Plains. There are a number of elephants about as well as the three families of bat-eared fox.

2

5

3

1 *In summer, Savuti becomes a birding paradise, with numerous bluecheeked bee-eaters, among many other colourful migrant species.*
2 *Dwarf bitterns are a rare sighting in this area, but we locate several breeding pairs.*
3 *A lioness lies casually draped in the branches of a dead tree.*
4 *Spreading its wings, a magnificent martial eagle prepares to launch into flight.*
5 *The wattled plover is found only near water, swamps or rivers.*
6 *The glossy Burchell's starling is one of the most commonly seen birds in the bushveld.*

6

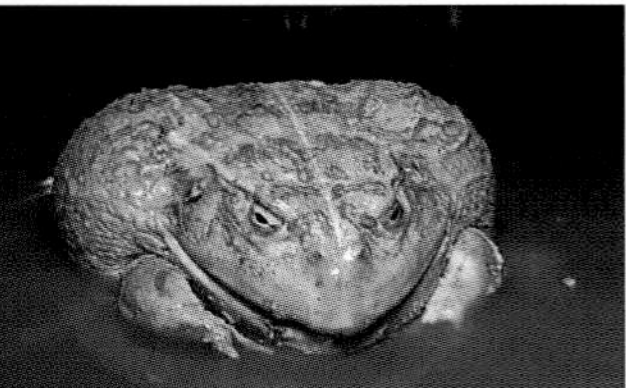

1

2

January 10 The roaring of lions wakes us in the early hours and we leave camp just before sunrise, heading in the direction from which the sounds had come. Pandani, the big Sethlare Pride lion, is less than a kilometre from camp, heading north towards Harvey's Pans. He stops from time to time, roars then stands listening for a response. Reaching the pans he breaks into a trot and runs across the plains, continuing through the mopane on the northern side until he comes to the main Savuti-Kasane road, which he continues to follow north. At the turnoff to the Savuti airstrip we find numerous lion spoor in the soft sandy track, and Pandani stops and sniffs at the ground then turns off into the thick scrub. It is too dense for us to follow through, so we race ahead to the airstrip, where we see Pandani passing by and continuing up and over the Magwikwe sandridge parallel to us. Later we hear from a pilot who has flown over the area that the Sethlare Pride are at a small pan to the west of the sandridge ... and that there are several large herds of buffalo there too!

We spend the late afternoon at the Harvey's Pan hippo pool, where Happy and a smaller hippo have taken up residence, then return to our camp soon after a spectacular sunset. While we are quietly enjoying a pre-supper drink, 15 elephants walk out of the bush opposite us, stroll up to within five metres of where we are sitting and stand silently watching us. For at least ten minutes we remain motionless while the elephants move all around us, using their outstretched trunks to sniff the ground where we have walked and our camp equipment. It is a magical moment and ends far too soon when the elephants turn and drift away into the gathering darkness, to be replaced soon after by the two hyenas that have adopted our camp as part of their nightly rounds.

3

4

5

6

1 *This huge bullfrog can attain a length of 200 millimetres and will take up to 28 years to reach full size.*
2 *We return to our camp soon after a spectacular sunset.*
3 *The late afternoon sun casts a golden glow over a lone elephant bull.*
4 *'Happy the Hippo' has found himself a mate, and they now occupy the pool at Harvey's Pans.*
5 *A colourful little grasshopper gleams like a tiny jewel.*
6 *One of the Sethlare Pride lions lies reflectively at the water's edge.*

Overleaf: *The gaunt skeleton of a long-dead tree is cast in stark relief by a stunning sunset sky.*

January 14

A redcrested korhaan *(Eupodotis ruficrista)* calling stridently at the roadside is our first subject of the day before we continue to Harvey's Pans to photograph the birdlife. The pans teem with a variety of ducks and waders and we settle down to photograph some redbilled teal *(Anas erythrorhyncha)* and a wood sandpiper *(Tringa glareola)*. There are several pairs of painted snipe *(Rostratula benghalensis)* feeding around the pans, and we have found that with patience we can make very close approaches to these normally shy and skulking birds. There is also an abundance of lesser moorhens *(Gallinula angulata)* which are also far from their usual secretive selves and parade around the pans quite openly.

Suddenly from the treeline nearby a cacophony of roaring erupts. Forgetting about the birds we rush towards the sound and find the Sethlare Pride in a state of turmoil. It appears that the two adult males are in the process of evicting the older sub-adult males from the pride. Two of these sub-adults in particular are nearing maturity and are showing good mane growth while a third is possibly of the same age group but slightly smaller. All could pose a potential threat to the dominance of Othello and Pandani in the pride, particularly as they are likely to band together and support each other in any power struggle. The largest of the three is already showing signs of growing into a magnificent lion, for he carries a huge head upon his broad shoulders and has a powerful and deep chest.

The three young males are inexperienced in these power struggles however, and they show it in their confusion at being turned upon by the big lions. The younger cubs run about in obvious fear, cowering submissively on the ground whenever Othello or Pandani come near. The two adult males growl and snarl fearsomely, and lash out cruelly at any of the youngsters that get in their way. Six of the lionesses meanwhile remain aloof, not getting involved in the power struggle within their pride, although one lioness shows some distress and joins the sub-adults, all huddled together in a show of solidarity, when a truce settles over the group. The youngsters repeatedly lick and groom one another, rubbing heads as if reaffirming their affections.

1 *The Sethlare Pride are in a state of turmoil as the two big males try to evict the older of the sub-adults.*
2 *The younger lions repeatedly touch one another, as though reaffirming their familial affections.*
3 *A redcrested korhaan calls stridently at the roadside.*
4 *Redbilled teal paddle about a small rainwater pond.*
5 *With patience we are able to make a close approach to the usually shy and skulking painted snipe.*

January 17

Savuti is looking very lush and green again, for it rains intermittently nearly every day now. The grass on the marsh is getting longer and very little game apart from the elephants remains there. We see the lions now and then, but they seem to remain across the sandridge much of the time, though we see them or their spoor most often around Harvey's Pans. Each time we see the lions the pride has been intact with the seven lionesses and nine sub-adults, though we have not seen Pandani or Othello since the morning of the big dispute.

After several rain showers throughout the day the sun comes out in the late afternoon and we drive to the marsh. We see a few big elephant bulls feeding on the marshlands and move nearer to photograph them, for the stormy sky behind them makes a dramatic backdrop when the sun breaks through in the foreground. We are busy with the cameras, when we look to our right. Further down the marsh we see a huge elephant herd moving out of the fringing woodlands. There are at least 250 to 300 individuals, by far the largest herd we have ever seen in Savuti, and they are all bunched tightly together and obviously distressed.

We start up and head towards them, driving carefully and trying to remain behind trees and intervening bushes to avoid spooking the herd. We are still approaching when suddenly overhead a large aircraft appears, and it swoops low over the herd. The elephants immediately panic and mill about, then turn back and run wildly towards the treeline again. The aircraft continues to buzz the herd several times, and in our anger at what is happening, we fail to photograph its actions even though on two occasions it is in the camera viewfinder low down above the panic-stricken herd. We later learn that the aircraft belongs to the Botswana Defence Force, a unit which in fact does sterling work in conservation and anti-poaching throughout the country but certainly blotted its copybook in our eyes today.

January 19

The rain keeps us awake for much of the night, thunder rolling around the nearby koppies, and we rise early and head for Harvey's Pans again, where we find a very tame and confiding lesser gallinule *(Porphyrula alleni)*, a first-ever sighting, or 'lifer', for us (p. 145). Though these birds are described as being 'solitary, shy skulkers' the lesser gallinule walks about in the open along the edge of the pan. I get out of the Land Rover and sit on the ground with a camera and tripod and the bird walks unconcernedly past me, at times so close I have difficulty in focusing on it! The lesser moorhens and painted snipe feed nearby and are also very co-operative again and we are amazed that we can have three shy species of birds all behaving like this in one place. Perhaps there's something in the water!

5

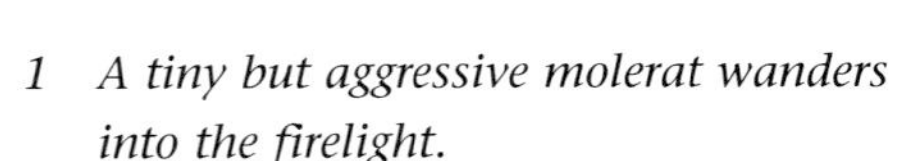

3

4

1 *A tiny but aggressive molerat wanders into the firelight.*

2 *Several whitefaced ducks stand alert at the edge of a temporary rainwater pool.*

3 *The striking woodland kingfisher is an insectivorous bird that does not fish at all!*

4 *A lone boabab tree towers over the surrounding landscape.*

5 & 6 *A huge herd of elephants moves out of the treeline onto the Savuti marsh.*

6

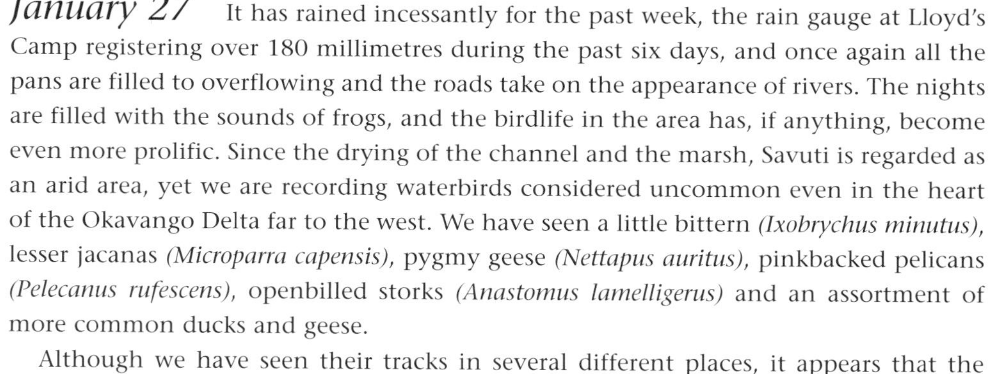

1

4

January 27

It has rained incessantly for the past week, the rain gauge at Lloyd's Camp registering over 180 millimetres during the past six days, and once again all the pans are filled to overflowing and the roads take on the appearance of rivers. The nights are filled with the sounds of frogs, and the birdlife in the area has, if anything, become even more prolific. Since the drying of the channel and the marsh, Savuti is regarded as an arid area, yet we are recording waterbirds considered uncommon even in the heart of the Okavango Delta far to the west. We have seen a little bittern *(Ixobrychus minutus)*, lesser jacanas *(Microparra capensis)*, pygmy geese *(Nettapus auritus)*, pinkbacked pelicans *(Pelecanus rufescens)*, openbilled storks *(Anastomus lamelligerus)* and an assortment of more common ducks and geese.

Although we have seen their tracks in several different places, it appears that the Sethlare Pride has split up. Although this may seem to be a sad ending to a magnificent pride of lions, it is in fact nature's way of ensuring genetic diversity and preventing interbreeding amongst related lions. Also, with the lean season ahead when hunting will become more difficult, it is likely that smaller groups will have more success in obtaining enough food for all pride members.

5

January 30

We hear lions calling near Bushman Paintings Hill but when we arrive see nothing but several sets of spoor. There is evidence that one or two lionesses are spending a lot of time in the area now, and we suspect that one of them may have given birth to cubs and hidden them. Lionesses usually secrete their cubs for four to eight weeks after birth and we know that they favour the distinctive rocky outcrops around Savuti for this purpose.

The bat-eared foxes on the Linyanti Plains have also disappeared, and we hear from a safari guide that the wild dogs had been chasing them. Although the foxes may have moved away from the area for a while, we hope the dogs have not killed them.

2

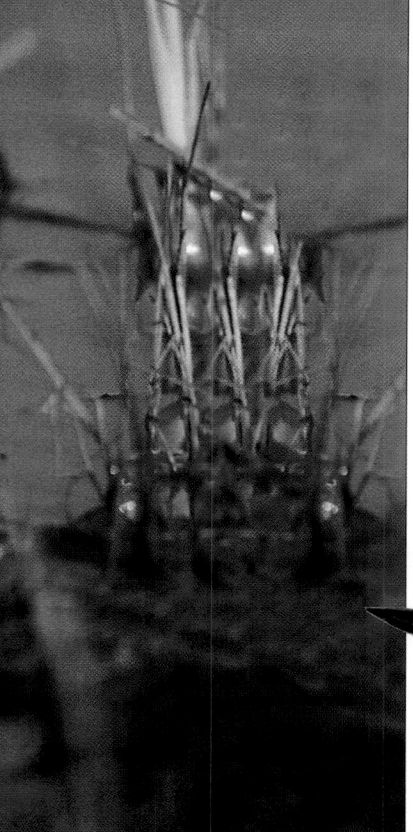

3

1 *A tiny threebanded plover prowls the fringes of the small pond.*
2 *A group of hottentot teal forages in the shallow waters.*
3 *Usually secretive and shy, the lesser moorhen parades around quite openly.*
4 *The ubiquitous blacksmith plover gets its name from its distinctive 'tink - tink - tink' call, like a hammer on an anvil.*
5 *The lesser gallinule is a first-ever sighting for us.*

February 5 With the abundance of waders, ducks and geese in the area it is hard to believe we are still in Savuti. We know that visitors who were here in September and October would have difficulty in believing this is the same place. We are concentrating on bird photography at present because of the lack of game, but even that is difficult with the wet and overcast weather, and we decide we should consider packing up and departing a few weeks earlier than originally planned. Even the other areas of the park are unfruitful at present, for there is so much surface water lying about from the rains that the animals are widely dispersed, many trekking far outside the park boundaries to summer ranges where food is more abundant.

Driving out of camp in the late afternoon we notice a band of clear sky above the western horizon under the thick clouds overhead and realise there will be some spectacular light conditions just before sunset. We head for the plains around Harvey's Pans but find little game there and continue to the Linyanti Plains. There are several kudu and impala out in the open, then we see a lone elephant ambling out of the surrounding woodland. It strolls out into the middle of the plains and heads towards a camelthorn tree where it hooks one tusk into the fork of the tree and stands at rest.

Just then the sun appears under the clouds and bathes the scene in a glorious golden light. The elephant stands motionless under the tree for some time, probably asleep, then awakens and begins scratching his shoulder and side against the coarse bark. He then turns and walks nonchalantly right past us, passing the vehicle within about two metres as the sun finally sets in a blaze of colour.

February 8 The rain has held off over the past two days and we have taken the opportunity to break camp and pack tents while they are dry, moving into Lloyd's Camp for our final days in Savuti. When we are not packing up or preparing our vehicles for the long trip home, we drive around the whole area visiting places which hold special memories and where we have had unusual encounters during our stay in the park. Although we have heavy hearts at the thought of leaving this very special corner of Africa, we realise that we can be more productive elsewhere, especially in sorting and captioning the thousands of photographs we have taken during our time here.

On the marsh we find three young elephant bulls in the company of several older bulls. The youngsters are all fired up and make several mock charges at us, then settle down somewhat and decide they should play with the Land Rover instead. They amuse us with their antics for some time before they tire of their efforts and wander off to join the others. We continue on our way and find a pair of knobbilled ducks *(Sarkidiornis melanotos)* in a small pond that is entirely covered with a tiny, bright green weed or algae. The drake poses perfectly for us (p. 150), turning this way and that as he preens his feathers, the green background setting off his black and white plumage well, while the duck paddles serenely about the pond.

1 *The elephant, standing motionless under a camelthorn tree, is probably asleep.*
2 *The sun appears under the clouds and bathes the scene in a glorious golden light.*
3 *Several guineafowl approach the water.*
4 *Although most of the game has dispersed now, many giraffe remain in the area.*

1

February 11 At Wild Dog Vlei we find an array of ducks and geese swimming in several ponds and even along the waterlogged road. There are whitefaced ducks *(Dendrocygna viduata)*, yellowbilled ducks *(Anas undulata)*, hottentot teal *(Anas hottentota)*, redbilled teal *(Anas erythrorhyncha)*, southern pochard *(Netta erythrophthalma)*, knobbilled ducks *(Sarkidiornis melanotos)*, spurwinged geese *(Plectropterus gambensis)*, Egyptian geese *(Alopochen aegyptiacus)* and pygmy geese *(Nettapus auritus)*. We spend most of the morning trying to get close enough to the pygmy geese for photography, but they disappear into the thick grass fringing the ponds whenever we approach.

After lunch we return to Wild Dog Vlei and find the pygmy geese again. This time we try driving the Land Rover into the middle of the ponds rather than skirting around the edges, inching forward slowly so as not to frighten the birds. Surprisingly, they show less alarm than when we stayed on dry land and we are able to make a close approach, the water lapping at the doors when we stop in the middle of the waterhole. The pygmy geese swim about quite unconcerned, and several whitefaced ducks paddle over for a closer look at us. Even when we start the Land Rover from time to time to change our position the birds barely glance at us, and soon they accept our presence and ignore us completely. We spend the afternoon in the 'duck pond', returning to camp after dark.

February 13 This is to be our last day in Savuti and to our joy we find most members of the Sethlare Pride scattered about Peter's Pan. Most of the sub-adults and three of the lionesses are there and they all look relaxed and in good condition. The big subadult male walks up to the Land Rover as though in greeting, and rubs his head against the brush guard on the front. He then walks around the vehicle, bites at the spare wheel attached to the rear door, and stands on his rear legs to grapple the tyre in his paws. It is an emotional moment for us, for we know we may not see these lions again for a long time and by the time we next return to Savuti some may even have died. We feel that we have been accepted by the pride during the weeks and months we have spent with them and this final show of affection is deeply moving, bringing lumps to our throats as we slowly drive away...

2

3

1 *The pygmy geese show less concern when we drive into the water to photograph them than when we stay on dry land.*
2 *Open wide – a lioness yawns wearily.*
3 *Two members of the Sethlare Pride.*
4 *Impala rams spar to establish dominance.*
5 *Play fighting among sub-adult lions prepares them for the real thing as they mature.*

Overleaf: *The knobbilled duck turns this way and that as he preens his feathers in the weed-covered pond.*

4

5

WHEN TO GO

Opinions on the best time of year vary along with visitors' requirements. The peak tourist season is generally May to September, and certainly this dry period is when game concentrations are at their best and most visible, particularly where there is permanent water. Although some camps and lodges close during the summer rains from November 30 to March 1, the wet season is also the green season, when most trees are in full foliage and the veld blossoms with an array of wildflowers. This summer abundance is also a time when many animals are accompanied by their newborn offspring and the summer migrants turn the region into a birder's paradise. The rains can, however, make the roads and tracks more difficult if not impossible to negotiate and inexperienced travellers, and especially those travelling without the support of other vehicles, should avoid the clayey mopane woodland areas around Nogatsaa and Tchinga, the Mababe Depression, the cut-line track to Linyanti and the Savuti marsh road. Even in the dry season the roads and tracks of Chobe can be all but impassable, as the thick, soft sand makes a sturdy four-wheel-drive essential.The section of the park along the Chobe riverfront near Kasane is open all year round and is accessible to ordinary motor vehicles with high clearance.

TOURIST FACILITIES

Chobe offers some of the best tourist facilities found anywhere in Africa, with options ranging from luxurious 'five-star' hotels through traditional thatched lodges, fully-catered luxury tented safari camps, guided walking trails, mobile camping tours and do-it-yourself options for the adventurous. Apart from the eastern sector of the park, around Nogatsaa and Tchinga, which is undeveloped and visited at present only by the mobile tour operators and self-drive tourists, the remaining areas — including Savuti, the Chobe riverfront and Linyanti — cater for all tastes and requirements.

Around the park headquarters near the village of Kasane, conveniently situated on the Botswana-Zimbabwe border less than an hour by car from Victoria Falls, both the Cresta Mowana Safari Lodge and the Chobe Game Lodge offer unparalleled luxury and comfort in magnificently designed and appointed hotels. Both lodges offer game-viewing by land and water, with a choice of large floating cruise barges and small aluminium powerboats.

For those looking for a slightly less sophisticated, more authentic safari set-up, the thatched A-frame cabins of Chobe Chilwero, positioned high on a ridge overlooking the Chobe River and floodplains where it can catch the cooling breezes, offers perhaps the best camp in the park. Chilwero also offers both boat and four-wheel-drive outings, led by some of the most knowledgeable guides in Botswana.

Top: *The lounge at Chobe Chilwero offers spectacular views over the Chobe River floodplain.*

Left: *Okavango Wilderness Safaris offer fully equipped mobile expeditions throughout the Chobe National Park.*

Far left: *A vehicle from Lloyd's Camp receives a thorough inspection from Savuti's famous bull elephants.*

Above: *Safari-goers from Selinda Camp enjoy a close encounter with lions.*

Right: *Linyanti Explorations offer walking safaris in the Selinda Concession.*

The Department of Wildlife and National Parks maintain a public campsite at Serondella, with basic ablutions comprising hot and cold showers and flush toilets, on a picturesque stretch of the river, though there are plans to relocate this campsite further west at Ihaha.

Mobile safari operators, such as Okavango Wilderness Safaris, offer an experienced guide, fully equipped Land Rovers, comfortable bow-tents and a mobile field kitchen for the duration of the excursion. The advantage of such a safari is that guests stay with the same guide throughout and are able to enjoy the excitement of seeing Africa in a manner similar to that of the typical safaris of 40 years ago. Apart from camping in the Chobe River area, Okavango Wilderness Safaris travel to Tchinga, Linyanti and Savuti as well as to the Moremi Game Reserve, Okavango Delta and Victoria Falls.

The Linyanti area proper has a brand new lodge at King's Pool and another overlooking the upper reaches of the Savuti Channel, operated for concessionaires Sable Safaris by Okavango Wilderness Safaris, while the Department of Wildlife and National Parks have a public campsite here too.

Further west, in the private Selinda Concession, Linyanti Explorations of Kasane have established two small tented camps. Selinda Camp and Zibadianja Camp both accommodate a maximum of 8-12 guests at a time in luxuriously equipped, authentic East African-style safari tents, each with an en suite shower and flush toilet. Being situated in a private concession outside the national park boundaries, these camps offer the added excitement of night game drives to spot nocturnal creatures, the freedom to travel offroad for close encounters with big game, as well as guided walking trails with an armed ranger and experienced guide.

Savuti offers three safari camps in addition to the Department of Wildlife and National Parks public campsite. Gametrackers Botswana, owned by the Orient-Express Hotels group, operate Savuti South and Allan's camps on the basis of 'hotels under canvas', while Lloyd Wilmot, one of the original characters of the area is the proprietor of Lloyd's Camp, which boasts that it offers guests a 'real African safari' experience. Lloyd's philosophy is that his guests should 'see, feel, hear and taste Africa' and he makes every effort to ensure that they do.

DO-IT-YOURSELF SAFARIS

For the more adventurous the option of a self-drive safari is a real alternative, either in your own vehicle or in a rented four-wheel-drive vehicle from one of the rental operators in Maun or Kasane, or even further afield. Car hire operators offer a range of four-wheel-drive vehicles in either two or four-seater options, and can supply fully equipped outfits including all the camping gear required, often including roof-top tents. Driver/guides are also available on request, for those unsure of their own offroad driving abilities.

Roads and tracks in Moremi and Chobe can test even the most experienced driver's abilities, and motorists should be aware that *all* provisions and fuel requirements must be carried with them, for there are *no* shops or petrol stations between Maun and Kasane, a distance of some 400 kilometres. National Park entry fees must be paid at the gates on entry to the parks. Only the correct amount in Botswana Pula is accepted, and there are no facilities for changing or accepting travellers' cheques, foreign currency or credit cards. Money can be changed in Maun or Kasane, either at the banks, hotels or lodges, but be prepared to pay a fairly high surcharge.

Prior to your visit to either Chobe or Moremi it is essential that you make advance reservations for camping at the Department of Wildlife and National Parks reservations office in Maun (signposted alongside the Department of Wildlife and National offices near the police station) or through Kasane Enterprises in Kasane. This new requirement often catches visitors unawares.

Campers should note it is extremely dangerous to sleep in the open and that tents should be used at all times. Malaria is endemic in Botswana and tents should be zipped closed against mosquitoes as well as predators, and proper malaria prophylaxis should be taken before, during and after the safari. Speak to your medical practitioner regarding the proper prophylaxis for this area.

An invaluable if not indispensable aid for the do-it-yourselfer is the excellent Shell Map of the Chobe National Park compiled by Veronica Roodt. (There is a companion map covering Moremi Game Reserve.) The map shows all routes and tracks as well as the better-known waterholes, and includes an illustrated bird and mammal checklist as well as a potted history of the park, along with general information. The maps can be obtained from most curio shops in Maun and Kasane, and from Riley's Garage, Maun and Kasane Filling Station, Kasane.

For motorists with vehicle problems, Riley's Garage in Maun is one of the better stocked service stations in southern Africa, and has comprehensive workshops. In Kasane options are more limited and while Kasane Filling Station can repair punctures, replace batteries and has a limited array of spare parts, Chobe Engineering have a workshop outside of the village on the road to Kazungula which may be able to help with more complex problems.

WHAT TO TAKE

Dress codes in Chobe are informal at the best of times, although guests staying at either of the two luxury hotels in Kasane may wish to include a slightly smarter outfit for evenings in their luggage. Winter days are pleasantly mild, though the early morning drives can be bitterly cold and a warm jacket or windbreaker is essential. Jeans, or shorts, and short-sleeved shirts suffice for the rest of the time, while a light sweatshirt or jersey may come in handy during evening excursions. Well-endowed ladies may find a jogger's or sports bra more comfortable while being jolted and bounced around during game drives. Travellers would be well advised to note that most of the camps and lodges offer a same-day laundry service — check when making reservations, for it can cut down considerably on the amount of baggage you need carry.

A good sunblock, lip balm and moisturising lotion are essentials, while a broad-brimmed hat rather than a cap helps keep your face and neck out of the scorching sun. For those with sensitive skins, a long-sleeved, lightweight shirt is a wise addition to the luggage. Beware though that people flying in light aircraft between camps are limited to soft-sided bags not exceeding 10 kilograms in weight, and these limits are strictly adhered to for safety reasons. Excess baggage charges could mean the cost of a separate charter flight!

A good pair of binoculars is essential to the full enjoyment of a safari, and there are numerous options from which to choose in the compact, lightweight range. Eight or ten-power are recommended magnifications for both game and bird watching.

Those hoping to bring back photographs of their holiday fall into two categories — happy snappers and the aspirant photographer. While there are countless point-and-shoot cameras on the market that will more than adequately record happy moments on safari, those wishing to return with close-ups of wildlife would be well advised to look at a SLR (single lens reflex) camera with a minimum of a 300mm lens. Any of the larger camera manufacturers are suitable, while one of the new generation of 75-300mm or 100-300mm lenses would be an excellent choice and provides that extra reach over the

Below: *The splendid thatch-roofed Cresta Mowana Safari Lodge overlooks the Chobe River outside Kasane.*

more common 70-210mm or 80-200mm. Add to this another small zoom in the 28-70/35-80mm range and you'll have most eventualities covered, even when that elephant walks up and looms over your vehicle! Films, whether print or transparency (slide), should be in the 100 or 200 ASA (ISO) range, with perhaps a few rolls of high speed film, 400 ASA (or higher), for the shot of those lions just after the sun has set.

There is a plethora of books available to enhance one's knowledge and enjoyment of a safari in the area. *This Is Botswana* (New Holland Publishers) by Peter Joyce and with photographs by ourselves presents an easy-reading overview of the country, its politics, economy and natural resources, including its wildlife. Birders would be advised to take along one of the excellent field guides available, such as *Newman's Birds of Botswana* or *Newman's Birds of Southern Africa*, both published by Southern Books. Slightly more comprehensive is the *Sasol Guide to the Birds of Southern Africa* (Struik) while *Roberts' Birds of Southern Africa*, only available in hard cover, is the comprehensive 'bible' of southern African birders, but is bulky and unsuitable as a field guide. There are numerous guides to the mammals, reptiles, insects, trees, flowers and so on available ... but remember that 10 kilogram limit. All of the camps and lodges should have a library of these reference works and other books, as does every vehicle in the Okavango Wilderness Safaris stable. Most of the lodges also have small curio shops which carry a limited range of books and videos for sale as well.

Below: *A vehicle from Gametrackers' Savuti South camp departs for an afternoon game drive.*

Bottom: *Guests relax alongside the pool at the famous Chobe Game Lodge, where Richard Burton and Elizabeth Taylor once honeymooned.*

USEFUL CONTACTS

AIR BOTSWANA
Sir Seretse Khama Airport, PO Box 92, Gaborone, Botswana. Reservations (Botswana): Tel (+267) 351921; Fax (+267) 374802. Reservations (Johannesburg): (+27-11) 447-6078; Fax (+27-11) 447-4163

AVIS 4X4 RENTALS
Tel (+267) 660258 (Maun) or (+267) 650312 Kasane

BOTSWANA DEPARTMENT OF WILDLIFE AND NATIONAL PARKS
Reservations: PO Box 20364, Boseja, Maun, Botswana. Tel (+267) 661265; Fax (+267) 661264

CHOBE GAME LODGE
Reservations: PO Box 32, Kasane, Botswana. Tel (+267) 650340; Fax (+267) 650280 or 650223

CRESTA MOWANA SAFARI LODGE
Reservations: Pte Bag 00272, Gaborone, Botswana. Tel (+267) 312431; Fax (+267) 375376

DELTA AIR CHARTERS
Direct flights from Johannesburg to Maun
Reservations: Tel (+27-11) 788-5549

ENSIGN AGENCIES
PO Box 66, Maun, Botswana. Tel (+267) 660351; Fax (+267) 660571

GAMETRACKERS BOTSWANA
Reservations: PO Box 786432, Sandton 2146, South Africa. Tel (+27-11) 884-2504; Fax (+27-11) 884-3159

KASANE ENTERPRISES
PO Box 55, Kasane, Botswana. Tel (+267) 650234

LINYANTI EXPLORATIONS
Reservations: PO Box 22, Kasane, Botswana. Tel (+267) 650505; Fax (+267) 650352

LLOYD'S CAMP
PO Box 37, Maun, Botswana.
Tel (+267) 660351; Fax (+267) 660571
Reservations: PO Box 2490, Fourways, Johannesburg, 2056. Tel (+27-11) 462-5131

OKAVANGO WILDERNESS SAFARIS
Reservations: PO Box 651171, Benmore 2010, South Africa. Tel (+27-11) 883-6255; Fax (+27-11) 884-1458.
E-mail: wildrsa@iafrica.com

RILEY'S GARAGE
Pte Bag 19, Maun, Botswana. Tel (+267) 660203; Fax (+267) 660556

Photographic Notes

Spending a year in a big game paradise like the Chobe National Park would be any wildlife photographer's dream come true, and we have been fortunate in being able to fulfil many dreams over the past 10 years. Two years in the Okavango Delta, a year each in Zululand's great rhino reserves and Namibia's Etosha, four years following elephants through some of Africa's best wildlife preserves and many months exploring East Africa's great game parks — Amboseli, Samburu, Masai Mara, Ngorongoro, Tsavo and Tarangire — all pale in comparison to the time we spent making this book.

Perhaps it is because Chobe, with its remote, forested eastern reaches around Nogatsaa and Tchinga; the swamps and papyrus beds of Linyanti; the scenic, game-rich riverfront near Kasane; and Savuti, the epitome of untamed wilderness, offers such incredible diversity to the photographer. Whatever it is, Chobe presents a constant stream of new images and challenges every day.

As with all photography, indeed all professions, the most important attribute is a thorough knowledge of one's subject and without this we could have the best equipment in the world (we do!), shoot hundreds of rolls of film and spend years on location without returning with worthwhile images. Add to this knowledge other essentials for success — a familiarity with your equipment and Patience (with a capital P) — and you have the right recipe.

To this end we spend many, many uncomfortable hours in our vehicle or lying in the dirt at the edge of waterholes, through heat and cold, rain and sunshine, seeking out our subjects or simply staying with them, learning their habits and hoping that something, anything, may happen that we would otherwise miss. Certainly there is such a thing as luck, but to rephrase the immortal words of champion South African golfer Gary Player, the more time we put into our photography, the luckier we get!

We use Nikon cameras and lenses exclusively, for above all else they are able to survive the rough handling and harsh conditions inherent in our profession, and we constantly refine our techniques and discard extraneous equipment. Our current battery of lenses ranges from 20mm to 500mm, which we find to be about the upper limit for effective and efficient use under African conditions. The lenses we find ourselves reaching for most frequently are the 80-200mm f2,8 zoom and the 500mm f4P and these are kept close at hand at all times. Also always ready for on-the-spot use, with loaded bodies attached, are 24-50mm and 300mm f2,8 lenses. We use Nikon F5, F4S and lightweight F801S bodies, as well as the fully manual, and excellent, FM2 for nostalgia's sake.

Although we find the built-in matrix light-metering and auto-exposure systems in Nikon's latest cameras to be almost foolproof, we use a hand-held incident meter and set exposures manually most of the time.

For night photography we use a pair of Metz 60-CT4s with Televorsatz flash intensifiers as well as a pair of Nikon SB24s, often switching over to the automatic Program mode on the cameras and letting the TTL (through the lens) metering system and in-built computers do some of the thinking for us.

Fujichrome Velvia and Provia 100 are our films of choice, though we will often push or pull the ASA (ISO) ratings of these films to vary our results or suit the conditions. All our film is entrusted to the care of Citylab laboratories in Sandton, Johannesburg and in over six years and countless hundreds of rolls of film processed we have yet to be dissatisfied.

We are firm advocates of the use of beanbags for steadying cameras and lenses and our favourite system consists of a simple platform fitting over the door or windowsill of the vehicle, with a heavy beanbag on which to rest even our longest lenses. Less steady, but often essential in panning with fast action such as cheetah in full flight, are steel brackets bolted to the doors of our Land Rover on which are fitted heavy-duty ballheads.

We try to keep the use of filters to a minimum, limiting their use to a selection of special Singh-Ray graduated neutral density filters, a polarizer and 81A and 81B warming filters which we use in conjunction with flash in night photography to slightly enrich the colours of the artificial light source.

The simplest advice we can offer budding wildlife photographers, however, is the old National Geographic adage: 'Be there!'

Index

Page numbers in **bold** type refer to main entries. Page numbers in *italic* type refer to photographs.